Keeping Faith

$\mathcal{W}$esleyan Doctrine Series

The Wesleyan Doctrine Series seeks to reintroduce Christians in the Wesleyan tradition to the beauty of doctrine. The volumes in the series draw on the key sources for Wesleyan teaching: Scripture, Liturgy, Hymnody, the General Rules, the Articles of Religion and various Confessions. In this sense, it seeks to be distinctively Wesleyan. But it does this with a profound interest and respect for the unity and catholicity of Christ's body, the church, which is also distinctly Wesleyan. For this reason, the series supplements the Wesleyan tradition with the gifts of the church catholic, ancient, and contemporary. The Wesleyan tradition cannot survive without a genuine "Catholic Spirit." These volumes are intended for laity who have a holy desire to understand the faith they received at their baptism.

Editors:
Randy Cooper
Andrew Kinsey
D. Brent Laytham
D. Stephen Long

Keeping Faith

An Ecumenical Commentary on the Articles of Religion
and Confession of Faith in the Wesleyan Tradition

D. STEPHEN LONG
with Andrew Kinsey

CASCADE *Books* · Eugene, Oregon

KEEPING FAITH
An Ecumenical Commentary on the Articles of Religion and Confession of Faith in the Wesleyan Tradition

Wesleyan Doctrine Series 1

Cascade Books
An Imprint of Wipf and Stock Publishers
199 W. 8th Ave., Suite 3
Eugene, OR 97401

www.wipfandstock.com

ISBN 13: 978-1-61097-899-6

Cataloging-in-Publication data:

Keeping faith : an ecumenical commentary on the articles of religion and confession of faith in the Wesleyan tradition / D. Stephen Long; with Andrew Kinsey.

xiv + 104 p. ; 23 cm. —Includes bibliographical references.

Wesleyan Doctrine Series 1

ISBN 13: 978-1-61097-899-6

1. Methodist Church — Doctrines. 2. Methodist Church — United States — Doctrines. I. Kinsey, Andrew. II. Title. III. Series.

BX8331.2 .L66 2012

Manufactured in the U.S.A.

For John and Marsha Brady, whose faith, generosity,
and constancy in the midst of life's trials have always inspired me.

Contents

Introduction

Growing up as a United Methodist, I often heard leaders of our church state, "We are not a confessional church." I am not exactly sure what they meant by that statement, but imagine my surprise when I discovered in my seminary course in United Methodism that in fact we have both a Confession of Faith and Articles of Religion and that teaching contrary to these documents is actually a chargeable offense according to our Discipline for both clergy and laity. This caused me to wonder: Why this deep disparity between what I received in practice as a United Methodist and what, I discovered, our church officially teaches? I do not think sinister reasons lie behind this disparity. After working and studying for more than two decades in United Methodist seminaries, I came to the conclusion that there are at least two reasons.

The first is the crisis in *theological* leadership in the church. Lay and clergy leaders cannot teach and lead people in the teaching of the church when they themselves do not know it. Despite our church's commitment to theological education, we do not actually teach much theology, and especially Wesleyan theology. We always manage to get sidetracked by the latest fad that will supposedly fix the church's problems. A simple diagnostic test will demonstrate this point. Ask your pastor if she or he can explain the doctrine of the enhypostaton. Then ask her if she knows her Myers-Briggs score. In my experience, clergy almost always know the latter but don't have a clue about the former, which presents how we can speak of Christ's two natures and yet of his being one Person who is the same Person as the Second Person of the Trinity. Since the latter is at the heart of the Christian mystery, one might think it is as important as knowing one's personality type, if not more so. The disparity between what we officially teach and what occurs in practice is not the fault of any particular church leaders, but it tells us where the priorities of our church, its leaders, and its publishing arms have been: on psychology and sociology but not theology. We do not know our doctrines, and because we do not know them, we cannot explain why they matter and why they are worthy of commitment.

A second reason for the disparity is fear that commitment to doctrine will bring with it an "inquisition." The idea of churches having trial after trial of clergy and laity for teaching doctrines contrary to the established standards in the church frightens many. I understand that fear and would not want to contribute in any way to such an inquisition, but I think it is unwarranted and misplaced and may even be related to the first reason for the disparity between our official teaching and practice. We fear that doctrine can only be used negatively and punitively because we do not know what it is. When we learn it, we discover that far from being negative, doctrine gives us positive knowledge of God that helps us see the beauty of God and God's creation and thus act in creation as we should. Doctrine matters because it helps us to give God glory, to love God and our neighbor, and to live as God intends for us. This is the purpose of doctrine. It is not to be used as a blunt instrument to force people into submission by threat and coercion. If it has been used for such wicked purposes in the past, we must not let the abuse of doctrine prevent us from its proper use. I trust that our church will not abuse it for such an alien purpose. Doctrine matters too much for us to refuse to be accountable to it because of such fears. While church trials must always exist at the outer edge of the church's life, doctrine does not serve a primarily juridical purpose. Instead, it helps us get about the most important task the church has—to speak well of God, to offer our praise and adoration rightly, and in so doing to sanctify God's Name and God's creation.

The following work offers resources to speak well of God and thereby know and love well God and God's creation. This is of necessity an ecumenical effort. The United Methodist Church did not invent Christian doctrine, and it contributes little that is distinctive or unique. This is a good thing, for unlike other disciplines where originality and uniqueness matter greatly, Christian doctrine depends on others and not the genius of some individual. Chesterton once said that Christianity is the democracy of the dead. In other words, doctrine depends on the communion of the saints. They help us speak of God as we should. We need to hear their voices. For this reason, this work is an ecumenical commentary on our Confession of Faith and Articles of Religion. It is ecumenical because it brings our doctrines into conversation with the broader Christian tradition. Doctrine unites us in a "communion," which is greater than the United Methodist Church or the Wesleyan tradition. Our doctrines show us how the God we worship is the same as the God worshipped throughout the Christian church. What follows is also a "commentary"; it is not official church teaching and does not pretend to be. Official church teaching is found only in the articles that begin each of the ten lessons. The commentary that follows is an effort to explain those articles and show why they matter. Inasmuch as the commentary helps make sense of the articles, it serves its purpose. If anyone mistakes the commentary for the articles themselves, then the commentary will have failed. Reading through the articles alone can be a dull exercise. My hope is that the following commentary will show the life present in the articles, and maybe even induce Wesleyans not only to read them but also to use them in their local churches.

I have divided the articles into ten foundational theological themes. Each of these themes will also be a volume in the Wesleyan Doctrine series. These themes lead us from a discussion of God to the Christian life and conclude with judgment. I have placed the articles within these ten themes, but I have not exhausted all the themes, nor did I comment on every one of the articles. Many important articles were omitted for the sake of brevity. The ten themes are:

1. God IS
2. The Trinity
3. Jesus Christ
4. Holy Spirit
5. Holy Scripture
6. The Church

7. The Sacraments

8. Justification and Sanctification

9. The Christian Life

10. Judgment

The Reverend Dr. Andrew Kinsey, a friend and colleague of mine, has made a valuable contribution to this volume in the form of the "questions for consideration" that follow each chapter (he also adds a comment on the whole book below). Andy is senior pastor of Grace United Methodist Church in Franklin, Indiana. His congregation is involved in a wide range of ministries, from partnering with public schools, to working with local agencies to address matters of poverty and unemployment, to overseas mission initiatives in Africa and Central America, to developing adult discipleship ministries. He is the Dean of the Wesleyan Connexion Project and the Indiana Conference Wesleyan Theologian, and participates annually in The Polycarp Project at Southern Methodist University. Whether this volume represents an introduction to Wesleyan doctrine or a review, I am sure that you will find Andy's questions to be both a challenge and a help to greater understanding.

Comments and Questions:

Steve Long's commentary on the Articles of Religion and Confession of Faith of the United Methodist Church provides a wonderful opportunity to explore the nature and purpose of the Christian life. Steve's division of the articles into ten "foundational themes" also supplies a helpful means of discovering the faith of the church once delivered to the saints (Titus 2). Throughout, there is plenty of insightful material to keep persons engaged.

The following questions are meant to assist in the exploration of the Articles of Religion and Confession of Faith. They have been created to help persons and churches understand more fully the importance of doctrine in the life of the church. While the current questions may not exhaust all the angles of the present commentary, they will hopefully help with opening up further study and reflection. The present commentary is an initial step in the process of ongoing catechesis, instruction, and formation.

Questions for Consideration:

1. What does it mean to say that the United Methodist Church is a "confessional" church?

2. Why do United Methodists, and Wesleyan Christians in particular, think there is a disparity between the importance of doctrine and the life of the church?

3. Describe the crisis in theological leadership in the church.

4. Why does doctrine matter in the church?

5. Upon what—or whom—does doctrine depend?

one

God IS

Articles of Religion: Article I: **Of Faith in the Holy Trinity**

There is but one living and true God, everlasting, without body or parts, of infinite power, wisdom and goodness; the maker and preserver of all things, both visible and invisible. And in unity of this Godhead there are three persons, of one substance, power and eternity—the Father, the Son and the Holy Ghost.

Confession of Faith: Article I: **God**

We believe in the one true, holy and living God, Eternal Spirit, who is Creator, Sovereign and Preserver of all things visible and invisible. He is infinite in power, wisdom, justice, goodness and love, and rules with gracious regard for the well-being and salvation of all men, to the glory of his name. We believe the one God reveals himself as the Trinity: Father, Son and Holy Spirit, distinct but inseparable, eternally one in essence and power.

Who is God? If the church cannot answer this question, it has no reason to exist, for we cannot worship what we do not know. The doctrines of the church are the teachings that help us know who God is. The word *doctrine* means nothing more than teaching. The Articles of Religion and Confession of Faith are the official teachings that let us know who God is. If we reject these teachings, we will no longer know God. Saddest of all, we would then be unable to worship God as we should.

1

These doctrines help us identify who God is. They are summary statements that come to us from Holy Scripture. They do not replace Scripture; to know God well requires searching the Scriptures daily, but these doctrines help us read Scripture well and thus know God.

That we know God does not mean we comprehend all God is. Any answer to the question, "Who is God?" will always need further development, for God is infinite and inexhaustible. Our language and thought cannot exhaustively say who God is. For instance, we are temporal finite beings, but as both our articles and Confession state, God is eternal. Because we are not eternal, we cannot know exactly what that means other than that God is not time-bound as we are. This demonstrates that sometimes our doctrines teach us more about who God is not, and this is what helps us understand who God is. They teach us not to speak of God as a creature. In fact, we are commanded not to make graven images of God or to turn God into a creature. If this occurs through wood, stone, language, or concepts, it violates this central command that Christians share with Jews. We must not invent a god who is like us. This would turn God into an idol, into a creature. God is not "one of us."

Every human person has a beginning, a middle, and an end. God is not like that; God is eternal. Every human person is a body that is composed of parts. God is not like that. God is without body; God is not composed of parts. Every human person is limited in power, wisdom, and goodness. God has no such limitations. Therefore our doctrines teach us that God is "everlasting, without body or parts and of infinite wisdom and goodness." But this shows us right away the difficulty in knowing God. How can we, who are limited, know God, who is not so limited? Two answers present themselves to this question. First, our knowledge of God will never come to an end; it continues to eternity. Second, the knowledge we have of God must come from God. Only God knows what it means to be eternal, without body, infinite in power, wisdom, and goodness; only God knows God.

We know God because God gives to us his Name and thereby invites us to participate in God's self-knowledge. To know God is to name God, but we do not get to name God anything we want. We do not name God because it makes us feel comfortable or empowered. We must receive God's Name, for this is how God shares his knowledge of himself with us.

But this is no easy task, for even the reception of God's Name is difficult for us to take in and acknowledge. Our doctrines seek to be faithful to receiving God's Name.

Receiving God's Name

Getting to know another person begins by knowing her or his name. When we first meet someone, we introduce who we are by telling that person our name. Exchanging names begins the process of knowing one another. Most of us received our names from our parents. Our names came as a gift from those who came before us and upon whom we depend. God's Name cannot be like that, for no one comes "before" God to give God a name. We do not name God as we name others, but despite the radical difference between God's Name and our naming, there is nonetheless also a similarity between God's Holy Name and the names we receive and give. All of these names come as "gifts." Just as we receive our names from others as a gift, so it is the case that we do not give God his Name, but receive it as a gift. This gift comes in a remarkable way; it comes as the most unlikely interruption on the most ordinary of days.

Moses is about his everyday business, tending his father-in-law's flocks, when God calls to him out of the burning bush. God addresses us through the material of everyday life, giving it an intensity it otherwise would lack. Moses turns toward this extraordinary sight, and God says, "Come no closer! Remove the sandals from your feet, for the place on which you are standing is holy ground. He said further, 'I am the God of your father, the God of Abraham, the God of Isaac, and the God of Jacob.' And Moses hid his face for he was afraid to look at God" (Exod 3:5–6).

On an ordinary workday, God appears to Moses and gives him a mission to be accomplished in God's Name. The mission is to bring Israel out of bondage in Egypt. God's Name authorizes the mission.

Moses remains unsure about both this mission and God's Name. So he asks God, "If I come to the Israelites and say to them, 'The God of your ancestors has sent me to you,' and they ask me, 'What is his name?' what shall I say to them?" God said to Moses, "I AM WHO I AM." He said further, "Thus you shall say to the Israelites, 'I AM has sent me to you.' God also said to Moses, "Thus you shall say to the Israelites, 'The Lord, the God of your ancestors, the God of Abraham, the God of Isaac, and the God of Jacob, has sent me to you': This is my name for ever, and this my title for all generations" (Exod 3:13–15).

Moses dares to ask God's Name. This is the beginning of Christian doctrine. It originates with Moses' boldness, his questioning: "Who are you? What is your name?" All proper teaching about God should take the same posture Moses takes before God. We recognize the sacredness of the task; to ask God's Name is to stand on "holy ground." But we are not to cower in fear; rather, we are to ask boldly, "Who are you?" God does not hide from us; God wants to be known. In response to Moses' question, God is not silent, but speaks: "I AM." This is God's Name forever.

"I AM" and the Names of God

The United Methodist Articles of Religion and Confession of Faith are not original. They are traditional elaborations of God's Name. According to our doctrines, God is one, living, true, holy, everlasting, without body or parts, of infinite power, wisdom, justice, goodness and love, who makes all things, who reveals himself as the Trinity. We will look at each of these elaborations of God's Name in turn.

God IS . . .

When God says "I AM," God establishes an identity between God's Name and the verb "to be." In other words, GOD IS. God is the fullness of being, and nothing that "is," nothing that exists, adds anything to God. At the same time, everything that is comes from God. God is not a static, inert substance located somewhere in space and time; God IS, which means that God is pure activity. Because "GOD IS," we cannot think of the category "God" as a genus that contains species. In other words, the term "God" is not like the term "animal." The latter is a genus term that contains various species—human, mammal, reptile, and so on. The term "animal" is a larger category that contains a number of smaller parts. God is not like that. God cannot be divided into parts. GOD IS. Or to put it in an even more complicated form: GOD IS TO BE. No being exists outside of God, for GOD IS. This could easily mislead us. For if God is the fullness

4

of being, and nothing that is can exist outside God, then does it not follow that everything that exists is, in some sense, God? The Christian answer is an emphatic "No!" God makes beings that are not God. These beings are called "creatures," and these include everything from the universe (or universes) to people to ideas to snails. Everything that is not God is creature, and yet only God IS. We explain this by appealing to a great mystery of the faith: if you add creation to God the result is not greater than God alone. In other words, God + creation is not greater than God alone. Because this is a mystery, it is difficult to understand and can never be fully comprehended. To say "GOD IS" assumes three things that might appear to contradict each other, but do not.

1. God is the fullness of being, the One, Living True God who alone is the source and cause of all other things.

2. The One, Living True God Who Is seeks to share being by giving it to things that are not God, which we call "creatures" and which possess their own independent existence.

3. The creation of beings that are not God does not take away from God's Being, for only God is "I AM."

God Is One, Living . . .

"God Is One" because God is not in a category that can be divided. Because "GOD IS TO BE," God is living. Living things are known by their ability to act; they can do things. God is the supreme actor who makes all other living things capable of activity. For some creatures, such as animals and plants, this action is based on instinct or natural processes. For human creatures, it is based on knowledge and will. But the source of all this action is the God WHO IS living. This is a restatement of the Jewish confession of faith, known as the Shema: "Hear O Israel, the Lord your God is One Lord" (Deut 6:4). To confess God as "One Lord" is to confess God to be our only God. There is no other God for us to worship but this "One" Lord. Jews and Christians have been willing to die rather than exchange the worship of the "One" God for other gods. The Romans were pluralistic and inclusive in their understanding of the gods. They were willing to incorporate many gods into their religion, but Jews and Christians were exclusive, for they had been commanded to worship only the Lord God, the great I AM, and not to bow down or serve any other gods. God is One.

God Is One, Living, True . . .

The one, living God is also "true." To be true means that one's actions (what we do) and one's being (who we are) are identical. Most of us creatures endowed with knowledge and will are not always "true." We learn to lie and be false. We put on appearances where we seem to be something that we are not. Our actions and our being do not always agree. We lack truth. God is not like this. Who God is, is what God does. Likewise, what God does is who God is. This is another way of understanding the Divine Name, which can be translated as "I AM WHO I AM" or "I WILL BE WHO I WILL BE." This reminds us that to know God's Name is not simply to figure out some kind of puzzle. To know God's Name we must follow God in the way God leads us, just as Moses and the Israelites did. We must leave the security of our own Egypt where we learn to be false, and upon leaving we pass through the waters and follow God's presence into the wilderness. For Christians, baptism represents this exodus from the deceitful and oppressive places in which we become comfortable to new life in Christ where we come to understand what it means to follow the GOD WHO IS.

God Is One, Living, True, Holy . . .

All our doctrines are for the purpose of making God's Name Holy through our lives. Jesus taught in the Lord's Prayer that the purpose of our lives is to make God's Name holy. He told us to pray, "Hallowed be thy name." This is the reason for God's revelation to Moses as found in the Ten Commandments, which are divided into two tables. The first directs us toward God, and the second directs us toward our neighbor. The first table commands proper worship and associates it with the right use of God's Name:

1. I am the Lord your God; you shall not have strange gods before me.

2. You shall not take the name of the Lord your God in vain.

3. Remember to keep holy the Lord's Day.

This first table reminds us that we are not to worship "strange gods" or turn God into some dead idol by making of Him a graven image. This is also what it means not to take God's Name in vain. God's Name is holy; we are commanded against using it for vain and empty things. This occurs when we treat God's Name as something other than a gift given to us and begin to think that we get to name God, rather than receive the Name from God. When we gather to worship, when we baptize, celebrate the Lord's Supper, evangelize, engage in mission and social outreach, we are to do it in this Name.

God Is One, Living, True, Holy, Everlasting . . .

To say, "There is but one, living, holy, true God" is another way of saying the Divine Name: "I AM." That GOD IS means that God is the most basic and most certain being. We tend to think that our own existence is secure and that God's existence needs to be proven, but this is to get things backwards. Our own being is less certain than God's. We are fragile and subject to accidents. There was a time when we were not, and there will come a time when we will no longer be. We are born and we die. God is not like that. God is everlasting.

God Is One, Living, True, Holy, Everlasting, without Body or Parts . . .

To say, "God is without body or parts" is to remember that God is not a creature. Creatures are bodies that have "parts." We are soul and body, and the two cannot be divided. Because we are composed of "parts," we are necessarily affected by others. No two bodies can be at the same place at the same time. When this happens, suffering results. For instance, I was once riding my bicycle when a large dog attacked my front wheel. Because the dog and my wheel are both "bodies" that cannot be at the same place at the same time, something had to give. My bicycle stopped, catapulting me onto the street. Suffering resulted; I broke my collarbone. Such suffering affects all creatures because we are bodies. God does not suffer like that. God cannot get into an accident, get hurt, suffer and die. This is why we say God is without body or parts and is everlasting. God does not have the kind of bodily passivity that all creatures possess. It reminds us of the difference between us. This is not to say that God does not have "passions" such as anger, wrath, love, and joy. But for God such "passions" are not necessarily suffered from others, as they are with us when we get into an accident or fly into a rage. God is not like that; God does not depend on others, but rather freely acts based on who God is.

Christian tradition uses two Latin expressions to explain this: *ab alio* and *a se*. *Ab alio* means "from others." All creatures come from something other than themselves. None of us "births" him or herself. Our "parts" come from others. *A se* means "from one's self." God is not from others; God is *a se*. We speak of God's *aseity* to remind us that God does not depend on others for God's being.

God Is . . . of Infinite Power, Wisdom, Justice, Goodness and Love . . .

Another way of saying that God is "without body or parts" is to say that God is "simple." All that we mean by this is that God is not composite. We immediately follow the claim that God is simple and without "parts" with "perfection" terms so that we do not misunderstand who God is. God's "simplicity" could mislead us into assuming that God is naïve or lesser than more complicated forms of being. Perfection terms prevent any such misunderstanding. Instead of thinking of "simplicity" as a lesser form of being that has not yet developed, perfection terms such as "infinite power, wisdom, justice, goodness and love," remind us that God, who is the fullness of being, is also the fullness of all that is good in creaturely life. These terms go together. We cannot play God's infinite power off against God's infinite wisdom, love, and goodness. Nor can we play God's infinite love off against God's infinite justice. In other words, God's infinite power does not mean that God is only some power that can be exercised at whim whenever God "feels" so moved by others. God cannot choose to be less than wise, good, or just, for God's power is not a power of choosing among competing alternatives, as it would be for us.

We confess that God is "all-powerful" or "omnipotent." But this power is unlike the power of a tyrant who acts only from will without being attentive to goodness, justice, or love. As the theologian Karl Barth put it, "God's freedom is the freedom to love." But God's infinite love cannot contradict God's infinite justice, and vice versa. Because God is "simple" and "without parts," God's power, wisdom, love, justice, and goodness are the same in God, although they will appear distinct to us. When God's love comes to us in the form of justice, it might appear as judgment. As we see in our Confession's Article XII, God's infinite love and justice do not prohibit judgment. When God's power and wisdom come to us in the form of love, it appears as mercy.

God Is . . . Who Makes All Things

God creates all things, visible and invisible, earthly and heavenly. Even "heaven," as well as all its inhabitants, is one of God's creatures. And the God who makes all things makes them in God's own image. They will bear characteristics similar to God's. Their being should be unifying, true, holy, and filled with power, wisdom, justice, goodness, and love, except for an important difference: God IS these things. Who God is and What God is are the same. Creatures are not God, and so we are not these things but are called to *become* them. We can only do this through God's grace. We can only participate in them; we cannot possess them otherwise than as gifts we receive and actualize.

God Is . . . Who Reveals Himself as the Trinity

We can only understand all the Names of God, from "TO BE" to God's "Infinite power, wisdom, justice, goodness and love," when we understand them within God's self-disclosure as the Holy Trinity. This is the great mystery of our faith, to which we turn next.

Questions for Consideration:

1. What are the primary purposes of doctrine?
2. What can happen when we reject the role of doctrine in the life of the church?
3. Who is God? Who is God not?

4. How can we know God? What does it mean to know God?

5. What's in a name? What's in God's Name?

6. What does God's Name do?

7. How or when does doctrine originate?

8. What does the statement "God IS" assume?

9. How were Romans, Jews, and Christians united and/or disunited in their understanding of God or the gods?

10. What does it mean to believe that God is living and true, holy and everlasting, without body or parts, of infinite power, wisdom, goodness, love, and justice?

11. What is the relationship between God's love and God's justice?

12. What other questions do you still have about who God is?

two

The Trinity

Articles of Religion I: **Of Faith in the Holy Trinity**

...And in unity of this Godhead there are three persons, of one substance, power and eternity—the Father, the Son and the Holy Ghost.

Articles of Religion II: **Of the Word, or Son of God, Who Was Made Very Man**

The Son, who is the Word of the Father, the very and eternal God, of one substance with the Father, took man's nature in the womb of the blessed Virgin: so that two whole and perfect natures, that is to say, the Godhead and Manhood, were joined together in one person, never to be divided ...

Confession of Faith: Article I: **God**

... We believe the one God reveals himself as the Trinity: Father, Son and Holy Spirit, distinct but inseparable, eternally one in essence and power.

Confession of Faith: Article II: **Jesus Christ**

We believe in Jesus Christ, truly God and truly man, in whom the divine and human natures are perfectly and inseparably united. He is the eternal Word made flesh, the only begotten Son of the Father, born of the Virgin Mary by the power of the Holy Spirit ...

Both the Confession of Faith and Articles of Religion begin by claiming that we believe in "One" God. Both also claim that this "One" God "reveals himself" in Three Persons: the Father, the Son and the Holy Spirit. How can God be both "One" and "Three"? That God is One and Three is the basis for the Christian confession of God as Trinity. Why must Christians confess that God is Trinity? The first and most important answer to this question is that Christians worship Jesus as God without confusing humanity and divinity. Because we worship Jesus, we must confess God as "Triune." If we fail to confess God as Triune, we will no longer be able to make sense of our worship.

Take a moment to look at, or think about, the structure of your church building. What is at its center? Most church buildings are structured so that our praise and adoration is directed to Jesus. Some symbol that represents him will be at the center—perhaps it is a cross, an image of Jesus, the eucharistic table where we celebrate the Lord's Supper, or a pulpit where we hear his words. These are all symbols of Jesus, and they invite us to turn toward him with our whole lives. They invite us to worship Jesus.

Inasmuch as our church buildings invite us to worship Jesus, they teach us that Jesus is God, for only God is worthy of worship. This is the witness the disciples bear in the Holy Scripture. Scripture depicts Jesus doing things that only God could do—for instance, Jesus forgives sins that were not directly committed against him. He is the author of creation. In fact, Jesus has an "authority" that can only come from God because it is God's own activity. John teaches us that Jesus possesses this authority because he was always with God, and was God.

> In the beginning was the Word, and the Word was with God, and the Word was God. He was in the beginning with God. All things came into being through him, and without him not one thing came into being. (John 1:1–2)

John continues by telling us that Jesus is the Son of God who reveals the Father's "glory" and "truth." God's glory is the manifestation of God's presence. This initially occurs in God's revelation to Moses through the burning bush. As God's "truth," Jesus bears one of God's most significant names. Recall that truth means that one's being and one's actions are identical. This is true of Jesus. What he does is who he is and who he is, is what he does. The way of his life shows us that he is the truth. Thus Jesus is the "way," the "truth" and the "life" (John 14:6). When he stands before Pilate after his arrest, Jesus tells him, "Everyone who belongs to the truth listens to my voice." But Pilate will not acknowledge who Jesus is, so he asks, "What is truth?" (John 18:37–38). This is a sad moment, because Truth stands before Pilate, but he refuses to recognize it. In case we miss the point that "'Truth" is another name for God, John bears witness to this one more time at the end of his Gospel. Thomas has refused to believe that Jesus is risen from the dead unless he sees for himself Jesus' wounds. Jesus appears before him and invites him to examine his wounds. In response, Thomas worships Jesus by confessing, "My Lord and my God."

When we gather as a church and worship Jesus, we stand in the tradition of the apostles, the first witnesses to Christ's resurrection. Our worship only makes sense if God is Triune. If God is not Triune, we Christians would be idolaters, worshipping a creature. This is strictly forbidden in the revelation given to Moses. We are to worship only God. We are not to worship any false gods, especially any that would be creatures. This is what the "pagans" do; it is idolatry. But here we come upon a difficult question. If we are not to worship creatures, then why is it that we can gather in Jesus' name, direct our prayers, praise, and adoration to him, and worship him? Jesus is a creature; he is "truly human," which is to be a creature. Does the fact that we worship Jesus make us idolaters? The answer to that question is an emphatic "No," but only because of the doctrine of the Trinity.

The doctrine of the Trinity has three important assumptions. First, like Jews, Christians believe there is only One God. As the first article stated, "God is One." We pray with all Jews the Shema: "Hear O Israel, the Lord your God is One." Second, Christians believe Jesus is God and therefore we can worship him without worshipping a mere creature. Third, Christians believe that the Holy Spirit is the One who gives us the ability to recognize and confess that Jesus is Lord and God. Because only God knows God, we could never know that God is Triune through our natural reason alone. The Holy Spirit graces us with gifts of faith, knowledge, and hope to know what we cannot know without the Spirit's assistance. These primarily come through baptism when we receive it with faith.

Jesus himself reveals the doctrine of the Trinity and associates it with baptism when he commissions his disciples after his resurrection.

> And Jesus came and said to them, "All authority in heaven and on earth has been given to me. Go therefore and make disciples of all nations, baptizing them in the name of the Father and the Son and the Holy Spirit, and teaching them to obey everything that I have commanded you. And remember that I will be with you always, to the end of the age." (Matt 28:18–20)

Once again we see the importance of God's Name. Now the three Persons known as "Father, Son and Holy Spirit" are also the revelation of God's Name. The mission takes place "in the name of" God, which is now Triune. No one could come up with this by her or himself. This is why our Confession states, "We believe the one God *reveals* himself as the Trinity: Father, Son and Holy Spirit." Because only God can know God's self, any knowledge we have must be a participation in God's self-knowledge. This is what the Holy Spirit makes possible for us, for God wants us to know him.

The practice of worshipping Jesus, of praying the Shema, and of baptizing in the Holy Triune Name is the basis for the doctrine of the Trinity. But the official teaching on the doctrine of the Trinity was not well formulated until two ecumenical councils of the church were held in the years 325 CE and 381 CE. These are called "ecumenical" councils because they represent the teaching of the whole church even to this day. Because of sin, the church divided into "churches," many of which claim to be the only true, universal or "catholic" church (the term "catholic" means "universal"). The first division occurred between the Roman Catholics and the Orthodox. Then the Protestants split from the Catholics. Protestants continued to split off from each other, and today we have so many Protestant sects that we can barely name them all. However, before all this dividing and splitting off from each other, the church held councils that Protestants, Catholics, and Orthodox continue to affirm. These councils set forth the proper teaching on questions such as who is God, who is Jesus, who is the Holy Spirit, and how are these three related to each other. The two councils that answered these questions were the First Council of Nicaea (325 CE) and the First Council of Constantinople (381 CE). Together they gave us the "Nicene Creed," which teaches us that God is one and three at the same time; that Jesus is truly God, who is one "being" with the Father; and that the Holy Spirit is also of the same essence or being as the Father and Son. Thus we can and should worship all three, and by doing so we still only worship the One God. Here is the text of the Nicene Creed. (All Christians should memorize these words and recite them often.)

We believe in one God,
the Father, the Almighty,
maker of heaven and earth,
of all that is, seen and unseen.

We believe in one Lord, Jesus Christ,
the only Son of God,
eternally begotten of the Father,
God from God, Light from Light,
true God from true God,
begotten, not made,
of one Being with the Father;
through him all things were made.
For us and for our salvation
he came down from heaven,
was incarnate of the Holy Spirit and the Virgin Mary
and became truly human.
For our sake he was crucified under Pontius Pilate;
he suffered death and was buried.
On the third day he rose again
in accordance with the Scriptures;
he ascended into heaven
and is seated at the right hand of the Father.
He will come again in glory
to judge the living and the dead,
and his kingdom will have no end.

We believe in the Holy Spirit, the Lord, the giver of life,
who proceeds from the Father and the Son,
who with the Father and the Son
is worshiped and glorified,
who has spoken through the prophets.

> We believe in one holy catholic and apostolic church.
> We acknowledge one baptism
>   for the forgiveness of sins.
> We look for the resurrection of the dead,
>   and the life of the world to come. Amen.

Most churches recite this creed every Sunday when they gather for worship. It is the most inclusive statement we have of the Christian faith; people from every nation, race, culture, and language on earth regularly say it. It binds Christians together in a common confession of the essentials of Christian teaching.

The articles in the United Methodist Confession of Faith and Articles of Religion assume the truth of the Nicene Creed. Our official teaching on the doctrine of the Trinity and on Jesus Christ restates much that is in it in different words. The Nicene Creed begins by confessing our faith in the One God: "We believe in one God, . . ." Notice the comma after "God" in this initial statement of faith. The three parts that follow this statement each confess our faith in one of the three Persons of the One God. So the structure of the creed is this:

> We believe in one God,
>   the Father . . .
> We believe in one Lord Jesus Christ,
>   the only Son of God . . .
> We believe in the Holy Spirit,
>   the Lord, the giver of life . . .

The One God is revealed in three Persons: Father, Son, and Holy Spirit. This is why our first Article of Religion states: "And in unity of this Godhead there are three persons, of one substance, power and eternity—the Father, the Son and the Holy Ghost." Likewise our first article in the Confession states, "We believe the one God reveals himself as the Trinity: Father, Son and Holy Spirit, distinct but inseparable, eternally one in essence and power." The terms "substance," "power," "essence," and "eternity" refer to God's oneness. The term "three" is only used of the "Persons" who are "distinct but inseparable." This fits with the results of the Nicene Creed. It teaches us that the Son is "of the same being" with the Father, as is the Spirit. This expression, "of the same being," means that they share the same "essence," which is also a sharing of the same substance, power and eternity. In other words, the Father does not precede the Son or Spirit in time or stature or ability; they always are together the One God. Because the Spirit is worshipped and glorified, the same is true for the Spirit. All three are God.

This is of course a great mystery. We do not know exactly what we are saying when we say it, although we do know what we are *not* saying. We are not saying that the Father is one third, the Son one third, and the Spirit one third of the Trinity. The Triune God is not divided into three parts. Remember from our previous discussion that God does not have "parts"; God is "simple." We cannot affirm God as Trinity if we do not also affirm God as simple. The three Persons are not three parts of God. In fact, we should also say that the Father is the essence of God, the Son is the essence of God, and the Spirit is the essence of God. And at the same time all three together are also the essence of God! Thus they are "inseparable." But the Father is not the Son or the Spirit; the Son is not the Father or the Spirit; and the Spirit is not the Father or the Son. Each is distinct. Another way to put this is to say that the Son is everything that the Father and the Spirit are, but the Son is neither the Father nor the Spirit (and the same is true for each Person.)

The doctrine of the Trinity defines what it means to be a Christian. One could not be a Christian and deny it. Why is it so significant? This is a dangerous question, and we must be careful in answering it. This is because knowledge of the Triune God is an end in itself; it is not to be used for something else. So if we say that the Trinity is important because it is useful for how we think about social relations, or politics, or the family, then we can unintentionally turn the Trinity into a means toward those ends rather than recognizing it is an end itself. In one sense, we should acknowledge that the doctrine of the Trinity is "useless." That is to say, we cannot *use* it for something else and thus subordinate God to another end. The Triune God is to be enjoyed and worshipped, not used. Otherwise we would take the Holy Name in vain, which means that we would use it for empty things.

Nevertheless, it is the case that we are made in God's image. Because God is Triune, we will find analogies to the Trinity in social relations, whether they be political, economic, or familial. This is primarily reflected in the centrality of love in our lives. The Trinity reveals to us that God the Father was never content to be an isolated, singular ruler but gives His "divinity" away to the Son, who "receives" it eternally. But the Father does not sacrifice his divinity by giving it to the Son; the Father gives his divinity away without ceasing to be fully the Father. Likewise the Father and Son give their common divinity to the Spirit, who receives it from them and unites them in that same divinity. They "communicate" with each other. As creatures made in the image of God, we already reflect this image in part; our life always comes as a gift from others. We are to receive it and in turn give "life" to others as well. But our life does not do this necessarily. We must become what we are—an image of the Triune God.

Questions for Consideration:

1. Why must Christians confess that God is Trinity? What are the implications of this confession for the Christian life, for the church?

2. What are the three important assumptions that we need to consider when dealing with the doctrine of the Trinity?

3. What is the significance of the ecumenical councils for the life of faith in the church?

4. How often do you recite the Nicene Creed? The Apostles' Creed? If your church doesn't recite the creed(s), what steps may it need to take to begin such a practice?

5. How do you understand the Trinity?

6. How does the Trinity define what it means to be a Christian?

7. What does it mean to suggest that the Trinity is "useless"?

8. What other questions do you still want to ask about the Trinity?

three

Jesus Christ

Articles of Religion: Article II: **Of the Word or Son of God,
Who Was Made Very Man**

The Son, who is the Word of the Father, the very and eternal God, of one substance with the Father, took man's nature in the womb of the blessed Virgin: so that two whole and perfect natures, that is to say, the Godhead and Manhood, were joined together in one person, never to be divided; whereof is one Christ, very God and very Man, who truly suffered, was crucified, dead and buried, to reconcile his Father to us and to be a sacrifice, not only for original guilt, but also for actual sins of men.

Articles of Religion: Article III: **Of the Resurrection of Christ**

Christ did truly rise again from the dead, and took again his body, with all things appertaining to the perfection of man's nature, wherewith he ascended into heaven, and there sitteth until he return to judge all men at the last day.

Confession of Faith: Article II: **Jesus Christ**

We believe in Jesus Christ, truly God and truly man, in whom the divine and human natures are perfectly and inseparably united. He is the eternal Word made flesh, the only begotten Son of the Father, born of the Virgin Mary by the power of the Holy Spirit. As ministering Servant, he lived, suffered and died on the cross. He was buried, rose from the dead and ascended to heaven to be with the Father, from whence he shall return. He is eternal Savior and Mediator, who intercedes for us and by him all men will be judged.

Who Is Jesus?

The doctrine of the Trinity states that Jesus Christ is "of the same being" as God the Father and God the Holy Spirit. But Jesus also shares "the same being" as humanity. This is why our church teaches that in Jesus, "Godhead and Manhood were joined together in one person, never to be divided; whereof is one Christ, very God and very Man." Our Confession of Faith states the exact same thing when it says, "We believe in Jesus Christ, truly God and truly man, in whom the divine and human natures are perfectly and inseparably united." This tells us who Jesus is. He is One Person in two natures. The two natures are divinity and humanity. But it is important to notice that they are united in "one person." In other words, the natures are not themselves united; they are not turned into each other. Human nature is not turned into divine nature; it does not take on the divine characteristics we examined in the first question such as everlasting, without body or parts, of infinite power and wisdom. Humanity remains temporal, bodily, composed of parts and of limited power and wisdom. Likewise the divine nature does not become temporal, bodily, composite, and limited. To transform the divine nature into human nature would be to make God mythological. This would deny the Creator–creature distinction. So we cannot say that divinity becomes humanity per se, nor that humanity becomes divinity per se. Divinity and humanity are not united in general, but the two natures become One Person—Jesus of Nazareth. Our second Article of Religion emphasizes this when it states, "the Godhead and Manhood, were joined together in one person." The Confession states the same thing when it refers to Jesus as the one "in whom" the two natures are united. The unity of the natures occurs not at the level of the natures, but in the one Person, Jesus. This is a subtle but significant distinction. It allows us to say three things that might appear contradictory, but as we grow in our understanding of the mystery of our faith, we realize they do not contradict each other. First, we confess, "Jesus is God." This is why we worship him. Second, we confess, "Jesus is truly human." This is why he redeems us; he shares in our creatureliness. Finally, we acknowledge, "Divinity is not humanity." This is what prevents Christianity from becoming mythology.

The language used to "describe" Jesus in our articles and Confession is not unique to the Wesleyan tradition. It comes from Holy Scripture as it is interpreted in the ecumenical tradition. The main language comes from the fourth ecumenical council held at Chalcedon. The deliberations of this ecumenical council gave rise to what has become known as the Chalcedonian Definition.

> Following the holy Fathers we teach with one voice that the Son [of God] and our Lord Jesus Christ is to be confessed as one and the same [Person], that he is perfect in Godhead and perfect in manhood, very God and very man, of a reasonable soul and [human] body consisting, consubstantial with the Father as touching his Godhead, and consubstantial with us as touching his manhood; made in all things like unto us, sin only excepted; begotten of his Father before the worlds according to his Godhead; but in these last days for us men and for our salvation born [into the world] of the Virgin Mary, the Mother of God according to his manhood. This one and the same Jesus Christ, the only-begotten Son [of God] must be confessed to be in two natures, unconfusedly, immutably, indivisibly, inseparably [united], and that without the distinction of natures being taken away by such union, but rather the peculiar property of each nature being preserved and being united in one Person and subsistence, not separated or divided into two persons, but one and the same Son and only-begotten, God the Word, our Lord Jesus Christ, as the Prophets of old time have spoken concerning him, and as the Lord Jesus Christ hath taught us, and as the Creed of the Fathers hath delivered to us.

The Chalcedonian Definition uses four words to gesture toward how Jesus is both human and divine; his two natures are united in One Person, without confusion (unconfusedly), without change (immutably), without division (indivisibly), and without separation (inseparably). Notice that these four terms are negatives; they tell us what Jesus is not in his two natures. He is not confused, changed, divided, nor separated. These terms give us the "playing field" within which we must speak about Jesus. They teach us to avoid two things. On the one hand, we must avoid confusing or changing the natures into each other. In the One Person Jesus of

Nazareth, divinity remains divinity and humanity remains humanity. But on the other hand, we must avoid so dividing the natures *in the One Person Jesus* that he becomes two subjects competing in one body. Thus the two natures are neither divided nor separated in the One Person. We take this so far that we can even confess that Mary is the "Mother of God." We confess these things always mindful that the drama of Mary giving birth to God occurs through the Person Jesus; divinity itself is without beginning and cannot be born.

All of this is perplexing and seemingly illogical, but then we are pointing toward something that is unique and beyond our usual categories of thought. What we are pointing toward is the second great mystery of the Christian faith. The first is the doctrine of the Trinity. The second is that of the incarnation. It is on these two doctrines that everything else in Christianity depends: its worship, ethics, and practice. The incarnation affirms that God can enter into that which is not God (creation) without ceasing to be God, and that God truly enters into creation, taking it into God's own life. This all occurs in Jesus' incarnation, life, crucifixion, resurrection, ascension, and promised return.

What Has Jesus Done for Us?

When God spoke to Moses, God said, "I AM WHO I AM" or "I WILL BE WHO I WILL BE." As we noted in the first lesson, this means that to know God's Name we must follow God in the way God leads us, just as Moses and the Israelites did. We can only know God's Name rightly when we follow along the way that leads to God. But who knows the way to God? When Jesus was heading toward his crucifixion in Jerusalem, he told his disciples that he would be leaving them and they could not follow, but he would make a way for them (John 13:36). This frightened the disciples because they did not know the way. To calm their fears, Jesus said to them, "I am the way, the truth and the life. No one comes to the Father except through me" (John 14:6). Jesus is the "way" into the life of God. Thus it is never adequate simply to know *what* he is. For instance, someone might understand and even confess that Jesus is truly divine and truly human, One Person in two natures, but to truly know this *requires* that a person follow him on the "way" to God that Jesus shows us. How is Jesus the way into God? We can see this when we think about six moments that characterize Jesus' life and ministry, which are mentioned directly and indirectly in our church's articles. We will divide up the articles into these six themes, gradually building up each theme until we return to the articles in their fullness.

Incarnation

The Son, who is the Word of the Father, . . . took man's nature in the womb of the blessed Virgin . . . (Articles of Religion)

He is the eternal Word made flesh, the only begotten Son of the Father, born of the Virgin Mary by the power of the Holy Spirit. (Confession of Faith)

The incarnation begins in time when the Second Person of the Trinity, the Son or the Word, is made flesh in the womb of the Virgin Mary. Both our articles affirm this, and our hymnody declares it. In his hymn of praise to the incarnation, Charles Wesley wrote,

> Christ, by highest heaven adored;
> Christ, the everlasting Lord;
> late in time behold him come,
> offspring of a virgin's womb.
> Veiled in flesh the Godhead see;
> hail th'incarnate Deity,
> pleased with us in flesh to dwell,
> Jesus, our Emmanuel.

The Wesleyan tradition offers this well-known hymn to all Christians, so that the profundity of our teaching can be mirrored in the beauty of our worship.

The incarnation is a creative act of God much like creation itself is. Mary's virginity is a sign that this is God's creativity. As Sojourner Truth (supposedly) put it, "A man had nothing to do with it." In fact, the church fathers understood Mary's virginity as a reversal and completion of the first creation. In the first creation, God brings Eve (the woman) from Adam (the man) without benefit of sexual reproduction. Jesus is the second creation in whom the first creation is reversed and fulfilled. Now God brings Jesus (the second Adam) from Mary (the second Eve) without benefit of sexual reproduction. Jesus represents the completion of creation. That is why Christians call the Holy Day on which we worship Him the "eighth day of creation." It is a new act of God's creating power.

The incarnation, however, is not simply the Virgin Birth. The term *incarnation* means "becoming flesh," and while this happens to the Word in Mary's womb, Jesus' entire life, death, resurrection, and ascension are all aspects of his incarnation, his being made flesh. They are how he becomes flesh. He does this in his life by taking on all the aspects of what it means to be human, except that he does not sin. He does this also by taking on that all-too-common experience of what it means to be human—death. Jesus gives himself over to death, even to be dead flesh—as we all will be—flesh that is taken down from the cross only through other people. He gives himself over to this ultimate state of powerlessness and is buried in the tomb. But then Jesus is bodily raised to new life, the first fruits of a new creation where God, human creatures, and all creation will live together in an intimate bond of charity. During his resurrection he teaches his disciples, and it is only from this resurrection experience that the Gospels are written. He then ascends to be with the Father and Spirit where he reigns in glory. This has important political implications, for Christ's victory relativizes all claims to power by nations and peoples. He promises to return again and complete the work of the new creation. All of this is part of God's incarnation—God taking on flesh and living intimately with it in God's own Triune life.

Jesus' Life

As ministering Servant, he lived . . . (Confession of Faith)

Jesus came not only to die but also to live. How he lived reveals to us what it means to be "truly human." Jesus not only shows us what it means to be God, but also what it means to be human. John Wesley explained this in terms of Christ's active and passive righteousness. Wesley explains Christ's "active righteousness" by affirming that "the whole and every part of his obedience was complete."[1] In other words, Jesus kept the law as God intended. Another way Wesley explained this was to say "he did all things well."[2] Jesus shows us what it means to live as fully human through his obedience. For Wesley, this obedience entails living a life that conforms to the beatitudes that Jesus himself gave us in the Sermon on the Mount (Matt 5:3–11). Jesus has the proper poverty of spirit and mournfulness. He is meek and hungers and thirsts for righteousness. He is pure in heart and a person of peace. All these things Jesus actively does through his life as a "ministering Servant." He shares this life with his disciples. In fact, his active righteousness can be ours. It is not only "imputed" to us, so that God sees *Jesus'* righteousness in place of our own, but it can also be "inherent" in us. It actually becomes *our* righteousness as well. For Wesley, this is the essence of the Christian life. "What is religion?" he asks. And he answers, "it is love which 'is the fulfilling of the law,' 'the end of the commandment.'"[3] This is why Wesley gave us "general rules" to follow. He thought we could "keep the law," but only through the power of grace.

In the above list of the beatitudes, I failed to mention the final beatitude:

> Blessed are those who are persecuted for righteousness' sake, for theirs is the kingdom of heaven. Blessed are you when men revile you and persecute you and utter all kinds of evil against you falsely on my account. Rejoice and be glad, for your reward is great in heaven, for so men persecuted the prophets who were before you. (Matt 5:10–11)

This final beatitude points to Jesus' passive righteousness. It is the result of his active obedience. Wesley defines this passive righteousness as "suffering the whole will of God from the time he came into the world till 'he bore our sins in his own body upon the tree.'"[4] Jesus not only actively pursues a righteous and obedient life, but he also allows himself to suffer at the hands of others. He suffers both the violence that is afflicted upon him at the particular moment of his arrest, torture, and crucifixion and also the sins of the whole world. Both Jesus' life and death redeem us. He

1. Wesley, *Works*, 1:453.
2. Ibid., 1:452.
3. Wesley, *Works*, 3:189.
4. Ibid., 1:453.

knows that "the hour" awaits him—the hour when he will give himself over as a sacrifice for the sins of the world. This is an essential part of the Gospel story and of our church's teachings as well. What does it mean?

Jesus' Suffering, Death, and Crucifixion

As ministering Servant, he lived, suffered and died on the cross. He was buried . . . (Confession of Faith)

. . . whereof is one Christ, very God and very Man, who truly suffered, was crucified, dead and buried, to reconcile his Father to us and to be a sacrifice, not only for original guilt, but also for actual sins of men. (Articles of Religion)

Jesus is a sacrifice not only for our guilt, but also for our "actual sins." If he were only a sacrifice for our guilt, then he would merely stand in for the punishment we deserve. Some Christian theologians see this as the primary purpose of the cross; Jesus suffers our punishment for us. But our Articles of Religion state that something more (not less) than punishment for guilt occurs on the cross—Jesus takes on our "actual sins." They become his, and he bears their wounds for all eternity. This is a great mystery, but it helps us understand a troubling passage in the Bible—Jesus' cry of dereliction.

When Jesus suffers the physical torment of the cross, he also suffers the torment of abandonment by the Father. He cries out, "My God, my God, why have you forsaken me?" This is perplexing. If the Father and the Son are one in essence, as the doctrine of the Trinity teaches us, then how can the Father abandon the Son? One answer is based on the teaching that the Son takes on the "actual sins" of the world. God is holy and cannot by nature participate in that which is unholy. In one sense we can even say that God does not know evil. When the Son takes on the evil of the world, the distance between the Father and Son becomes unbearable. The Father must turn from the Son, who even descends into hell—the ultimate act of powerlessness in being-made-flesh. This is a moment of "high drama." We remember it on Holy Saturday, the one day in the church year when we do not preach the Gospel or celebrate the sacrament. For it appears that, with the Son's abandonment by the Father, sin and evil silence even God.

After Good Friday, we leave the church in silence, but we can do this in hope because we know the silence gives way in light of the resurrection. Otherwise we could only proclaim the words of despair, "God is dead and we have killed him."

Jesus' Resurrection

As ministering Servant, he lived, suffered and died on the cross. He was buried, rose from the dead . . . (Confession of Faith)

Christ did truly rise again from the dead, and took again his body, with all things appertaining to the perfection of man's nature . . . (Articles of Religion)

Can the Father truly abandon the Son even when he takes upon himself the "actual sins" of the world? If Jesus' body remained in the tomb, if the story ended with his burial and death, then evil and sin would have the last word. There would be no reason to preach, no reason to celebrate the sacraments, no reason for the disciples to bear witness. But the bond of the Holy Spirit, who proceeds from the Father and the Son, cannot be broken. That God cannot know evil is a mystery, but there is a deeper one yet, and that is the mystery of God's love. It overcomes sin, death, and the devil, so that the cry of dereliction turns into a cry of exaltation:

> And being found in human form he humbled himself and became obedient unto death, even death on a cross. Therefore God has highly exalted him and bestowed on him the Name which is above every name, that at the name of Jesus every knee should bow, in heaven and on earth and under the earth, and every tongue confess that Jesus Christ is Lord to the glory of God the Father. (Phil 2:8–11)

Our actual sins are taken into the very life of God and redeemed. The seriousness of this teaching should not be underestimated. Every act of violence, every betrayal, every deceit, every instance of manipulation, abuse, sloth, cowardice, pride, lust, and greed, and even our indifference towards others is taken into Christ's body and redeemed. This means that he bears the wounds of sin throughout eternity for our sake. If our sins are not to have the last word, then they must be overcome by life, not death. Death is not redemptive. Life is. For this reason, Jesus must be *bodily* raised from the dead; this is what our church teaches, and it is the only way to believe in the resurrection. He "took again his body, with all things appertaining to the perfection of man's nature." When the church teaches that he "took again his body," it teaches us that the tomb was empty. The resurrection is not just an idea that life goes on in some way after death; it is a full-bodied reality that reminds us that God seeks a place for *creation* in God's own Triune life. To be a creature is to be embodied. If the resurrection does not include "bodies," then creation will not be redeemed. Christ's bodily resurrection is the first fruits of the new creation. Indeed, this resurrection is not a mere resuscitation of a dead corpse; it is not the Night of the Living Dead! But no one in the church's official teaching tradition has ever taught that it was. Christ's risen body is odd. He shows up behind locked doors and asks for a fish. He is both recognized by others and not recognized. He seems limited by space and time at the same time that he transcends them. In fact, the nature of his risen body is so odd that it has always made me think that if the disciples were simply making it up, they should have done a better job. But they were proclaiming a mystery. God does not redeem us from creatureliness, but *in* it, for it is "good."

Jesus' Ascension

As ministering Servant, he lived, suffered and died on the cross. He was buried, rose from the dead and ascended to heaven to be with the Father . . . (Confession of Faith)

Christ did truly rise again from the dead, and took again his body, with all things appertaining to the perfection of man's nature, wherewith he ascended into heaven . . . (Articles of Religion)

Jesus' resurrection is not the end of the story. He also "ascends" to the Father. The Acts of the Apostles tells us the story. Jesus has been with the disciples since his resurrection. The disciples ask him a question: "Lord, will you at this time restore the kingdom to Israel?" (1:6). This is a good question, because the resurrection is the beginning of the restoration of God's creation when a new Jerusalem will be the center of a redeemed creation. But Jesus tells them, "It is not for you to know times or seasons which the Father has fixed by his own authority. But you shall receive power when the Holy Spirit has come upon you; and you shall be my witnesses in Jerusalem and in all Judea and Samaria and to the end of the earth" (1:7–8). Then Scripture tells us, "And when he had said this, as they were looking on, he was lifted up, and a cloud took him out of their sight" (2:6–9). In the ascension, the risen Jesus is no longer present to the disciples as he was prior to the ascension. He is of course still present to us through the Holy Spirit, who works through the Word and in the Sacrament, but in one sense all our churches are "empty tombs" where we go to wait for the Ascended Christ to return. During this time, we are to be witnesses throughout the world. The time between Christ's ascension and his return is the time of witness.

Jesus' Return

As ministering Servant, he lived, suffered and died on the cross. He was buried, rose from the dead and ascended to heaven to be with the Father, from whence he shall return. He is eternal Savior and Mediator, who intercedes for us and by him all men will be judged.

Christ did truly rise again from the dead, and took again his body, with all things appertaining to the perfection of man's nature, wherewith he ascended into heaven, and there sitteth until he return to judge all men at the last day.

Until he returns, we wait. But for what are we waiting? We await judgment. We will examine this more closely when we look at Article XII of our Confession of Faith. Suffice it to say now that the judgment we await is not awaiting punishment. It is waiting for that day when violence, greed, deceit, and betrayal no longer have power over our lives, when they will be decisively judged so that they cannot rule. We await the vision of the "new heaven and new earth," of which Christ's risen body is the first fruits. We are given a glimpse of this vision in the book of Revelation:

> Then I saw a new heaven and a new earth; for the first heaven and the first earth had passed away, and the sea was no more. And I saw the holy city, new Jerusalem, coming down out of heaven from God, prepared as a bride adorned for her husband . . . And I saw no

temple in the city, for its temple is the Lord God the Almighty and the Lamb. And the city has no need of sun or moon to shine upon it, for the glory of God is its light, and its lamp is the Lamb. By its light shall the nations walk; and the kings of the earth shall bring their glory into it, and its gates shall never be shut by day—and there shall be no night there; they shall bring into it the glory and the honor of the nations. But nothing unclean shall enter it, nor any one who practices abomination or falsehood, but only those who are written in the Lamb's book of life. (Rev 21:1–2, 22–27)

Questions for Consideration:

1. Who is Jesus Christ?

2. What are the three things about Jesus Christ that appear contradictory but are necessary to vital faith and knowledge of God?

3. What must we avoid when speaking about Jesus?

4. What has Jesus done for us?

5. How is Jesus the way into God?

    a. Incarnation

        i. What is the incarnation?

        ii. Read: John 1:1–5

        iii. What are the implications of the incarnation for political, economic, and family life?

    b. Jesus' Life

        i. Why is "active righteousness" important to the Christian life?

        ii. What is "imputed" righteousness?

        iii. What is "inherent" righteousness?

        iv. What is "passive" righteousness?

        v. Read: Philippians 2:5–11

    c. Jesus' Suffering, Death, and Crucifixion

        i. What does it mean to believe that Jesus is not only a sacrifice for our guilt but also for our actual sins?

    ii. Read: Mark 15:1–47

    iii. What does it mean to say that Jesus took into his body our sins?

d. Jesus' Resurrection

    i. What does it mean to say that Jesus was raised bodily from the grave?

    ii. What does it mean to believe that Jesus "took again his body"?

    iii. How are resurrection and creation related?

    iv. Read: Mark 16:1–8

e. Jesus' Ascension

    i. How is the church an "empty tomb" waiting for Christ to return?

    ii. What is the ascension?

    iii. When is the ascension celebrated in your church?

    iv. Read: Acts 1:2–8

f. Jesus' Return

    i. What is the Day we await?

    ii. What popular misconceptions are there about Jesus' return?

    iii. How shall Christians live between now and that Day?

    iv. Read: Revelation 21:22–27

four

The Holy Spirit

Who Is the Holy Spirit?

We already determined that the Holy Spirit (sometimes referred to as the Holy Ghost) is one of the Three Persons of the Trinity and also the fullness of God's essence. The Spirit is thus "one in being with the Father and the Son," and at the same time distinct from each. The Father, Son, and Spirit are not three parts of the Trinity; each is both a distinct Person and the essence of God. This why we say that God is three in one and one in three. The unity reminds us that the Spirit, like the other two Persons of the Trinity, is God, and therefore worthy of our worship. When we praise, we can address our praise to the Spirit. Likewise when we pray, we can pray directly to the Spirit. The church proclaims the Holy Spirit to be God because of both Scripture and worship.

Christian doctrine helps us worship God well. Likewise, Christian worship helps us understand what we should teach. This is an ancient principle in the church, which states that the "law of praying is the law of believing," and the "law of believing is the law of praying." This principle is found in a Latin expression: *lex orandi, lex credendi. Lex orandi* means "the law of praying," while *lex credendi* means "the law of believing." As the Methodist theologian Geoffrey Wainright has noted, this expression can be read in two ways; it "makes the rule of prayer a norm for belief," but it also suggests that "what must be believed governs what may and should be prayed." The result is that "worship influences doctrine and doctrine worship."[1] This principle made it necessary first for the church to confess, "we believe in the Holy Spirit, the Lord, the giver of life, who proceeds from the Father and the Son." This was necessary because proper worship demanded it. Now the doctrine of the Holy Spirit governs how we can properly worship. If we deny the divinity of the Holy Spirit, we could neither worship well nor be true Christian disciples. This is why we pray and sing for the Spirit to illumine us. This is present in our prayer before reading Scripture, where we pray to the Spirit as Lord and say, "Lord, open our hearts and minds by the power of your Holy Spirit, that, as the Scriptures are read and your Word proclaimed, we may hear with joy what you say to us today."[2]

Why does proper worship require that we confess the Holy Spirit is as fully God as the Father and the Son? St. Basil the Great, who lived from 330–379 CE and helped the church craft its language to speak of God, put forth one of the central reasons. He wrote a famous treatise, called *On the Holy Spirit*, that maintained the tradition of speaking of the Holy Spirit as God against those who wanted to think of the Spirit as somehow less than God. Basil emphasized that we would not be able to offer God praise and glory properly if we did not recognize that we praise and glorify God by equating all three Persons of the Trinity. We praise and glorify God by saying, "Glory be to the Father and to the Son and to the Holy Spirit." This

1. Wainwright, *Doxology*, 218.
2. *United Methodist Hymnal*, 6.

is an ancient expression of our prayer of praise, known as a doxology. If we fail to recognize that all three Persons refer in the same way to God while at the same time maintaining their distinctness, then we could not praise God as we should. Because the central task of our lives is to praise and glorify God, this would have dire consequences for understanding the reason for our own creaturely existence.

The Holy Spirit is the object of our worship, prayer, and praise. At the same time, the Spirit is the origin and means of our prayers. Charles Wesley's hymn of prayer to the Holy Spirit, "Come, Holy Ghost, Our Hearts Inspire," brings out this threefold reality of the Spirit's work. The Spirit receives our prayers, originates our prayers, and sustains our prayers:

> Come, Holy Ghost, our hearts inspire,
> let us thine influence prove;
> source of the old prophetic fire,
> fountain of life and love.

> Come, Holy Ghost (for moved by thee
> the prophets wrote and spoke),
> unlock the truth, thyself the key,
> unseal the sacred book.

> Expand thy wings, celestial Dove,
> brood o'er our nature's night;
> on our disordered spirits move,
> and let there now be light.

> God, through the Spirit we shall know
> if thou within us shine,
> and sound, with all thy saints below,
> the depths of love divine.[3]

Charles Wesley's hymn directly addresses the Holy Spirit as someone who acts. The Spirit has "divine agency," which means that what the Spirit does is what God does. God and the Spirit are one and the same. This is a key reason why the Nicene Creed also insists that the Spirit is God.

---

3. *United Methodist Hymnal*, 603.

The creed states that we believe "in the Holy Spirit, the Lord, the giver of life, who proceeds from the Father and the Son, who with the Father and the Son is worshiped and glorified, who has spoken through the prophets." Who can give life but God? Who can speak through the prophets? Who is worthy of worship and of being glorified? Who else is Lord? The Spirit is all these things, because the Spirit is God.

We must be careful to avoid two common errors in speaking about the Holy Spirit. The first is to deny that the Holy Spirit is God, even if this means that we think of the Spirit as a quasi-god who manifests God's power but is not fully God. The Spirit is more than just a manifestation of God's power. The second is to see the Father, the Son and the Spirit as three modes of God where God first appears in the mode of the Father, then in the mode of the Son, and finally in the mode of the Spirit. This error states that when God appears as Father, God is neither Son nor Spirit; when God appears as Son, God does not remain Father and is not yet Spirit; and when God appears as Spirit, God is no longer Father and Son. In other words, God the Father "morphs" into God the Son, who then "morphs" into the Holy Spirit. These are ancient errors that the church has always rejected.

The second error gives rise to a faulty division of history in terms of various dispensations. The first dispensation is that of the Father, and is usually thought to be the time of the Old Testament. The second is the dispensation of the Son, the time of the New Testament. The third is of the Holy Spirit and is found in modern times when both the Old and New Testament covenants are superseded by a new "spiritual" covenant that exists without the church or a community of faith. This dispensationalist form of thinking often misleads people into claiming that they can be "spiritual" without being "religious." In other words, they have no need of the church, the Scriptures, or the Christian tradition because they have a relationship with the Holy Spirit and so no longer need these things. It is wrong because it sets the Father, the Son, and the Spirit against each other. Each must "overcome" the other Persons in order for God to become God. This would make it necessary for God to be in conflict with God's self for the sake of our redemption, and it would reject most of those names for God that we mentioned in the first lesson.

What Does the Spirit Do?

The Spirit is God not only because proper worship demands that we confess the Spirit as such, but even more because Holy Scripture does. We see this most clearly in the Gospel of John where once again Jesus speaks of his "going away" from the disciples because of his impending crucifixion and then ascension. He will no longer be with the disciples in the same bodily form that he was with them in his pre-resurrection and pre-ascension life. Rather than this being a cause for alarm and sadness, he tells the disciples that it is actually to their "advantage" that he go away, for otherwise "the Counselor will not come to you; but if I go, I will send him to you" (John 16:7). The Counselor who is coming to them is the Holy Spirit. Then Jesus explains what the Counselor will do:

> And when he comes, he will convince the world concerning sin and righteousness and judgment; concerning sin, because they do not believe in me; concerning righteousness, because I go to the Father, and you will see me no more; concerning judgment, because the ruler of this world is judged. I have yet many things to say to you, but you cannot bear them now. When the Spirit of truth comes, he will guide you into all the truth; for he will not speak on his own authority, but whatever he hears he will speak, and he will declare to you the things that are to come. He will glorify me, for he will take what is mine and declare it to you. All that the Father has is mine; therefore I said that he will take what is mine and declare it to you. (John 16:8–15)[4]

The Holy Spirit reveals what the Father makes known to the Son. The Spirit can only do this because the Spirit shares the fullness of God with the Father and the Son.

The Spirit "convinces," "guides," "speaks," "declares," and "glorifies." The Spirit does these actions with specific attention to judgment, righteousness, truth, and language. The Spirit convinces us of sin and judges it in our lives. This is not for the purpose of condemnation, but to lead us into righteousness. The Holy Spirit makes the church holy by guiding us into the life of God. The Spirit "hears" the conversation between the Father and Son and manifests it in the church and the world. If we "speak" or "hear" the Word of God, it is because the Spirit makes such speaking

---

4. See Geoffrey Wainwright's "The Holy Spirit," 278.

and hearing possible. This is sometimes done with ecstatic manifestations that appear unruly. At other times, all appears in good order. In fact, often when we pray, the leader begins with the statement, "The Lord be with you," to which the church responds, "And also with you." "The Lord" in this exchange refers to the "Holy Spirit," who is the "Lord" and "giver of life." This is an important exchange because it reminds us that even if everything is done in the proper order in the life of the church—even if persons presiding are properly ordained and preachers properly credentialed, and the Discipline obeyed and respected—it is still insufficient unless the Holy Spirit is present in our common life. So we invoke the Spirit's presence: "The Lord be with you." The Spirit undergirds our speech and makes it truthful. This happens when our freely expressed words and actions correspond to how God intends the world to be. The Spirit is the Spirit of truth, which means that the Spirit is also the Spirit of Jesus, who is the truth made known to the world.

Jesus and the Holy Spirit should never be separated, even though they are distinct. They are distinct in their identity. In fact, an interesting "inversion" takes place in the relationship between them. When Jesus' ministry begins, it is the Holy Spirit who inaugurates it. John the Baptist prophesies that One is coming after him who is greater than he. His greatness will be shown in that He will baptize with the Holy Spirit, whereas John only baptizes with water. Yet when Jesus meets John at the Jordan River, Jesus accepts John's baptism. This baptism is also done in the Holy Spirit; this is when the Spirit comes upon Jesus and prepares him for ministry.

> Now when all the people were baptized, and when Jesus also had been baptized and was praying, the heaven was opened, and the Holy Spirit descended upon him in bodily form, as a dove, and a voice came from heaven, "Thou art my beloved Son; with thee I am well pleased." (Luke 3:21–22)

After this Jesus begins his ministry, which represents the ministry of Israel itself. For just as Israel wandered forty years in the desert and faced temptations, so Jesus wanders forty days in the wilderness and faces similar temptations. It is the Spirit who leads him during this time.

> And Jesus, full of the Holy Spirit, returned from the Jordan, and was led by the Spirit for forty days in the wilderness, tempted by the devil. (Luke 4:1–2)

Although the Spirit leads Jesus in his ministry, after his Resurrection, Jesus sends the Holy Spirit upon the church so that the church can continue his ministry. This occurs at Pentecost and represents the "inversion" between them. The Spirit makes Jesus' mission possible from the incarnation through the ascension. Jesus then sends the Spirit on the church to continue his mission until he comes again.

When we discussed the ascension in lesson three, we noticed that Jesus promised to send his disciples the Holy Spirit who would help them witness to Jesus. After Jesus ascended, the disciples gathered together on the day of Pentecost, which was a Jewish festival. Scripture recounts the sending of the Spirit, who now empowers the disciples to carry on Jesus' ministry in Acts 2.

> When the day of Pentecost had come, they were all together in one place. And suddenly a sound came from heaven like the rush of a mighty wind, and it filled all the house where they were sitting. And there appeared to them tongues as of fire, distributed and resting on each one of them. And they were all filled with the Holy Spirit and began to speak in other tongues, as the Spirit gave them utterance. (Acts 2:1–4)

This resulted, as the presence of the Spirit often does, in ecstatic manifestations of God's power and glory. We should not fear these ecstatic manifestations; however, the true Pentecostal miracle is never found in displays of power for their own sake. The true Pentecostal miracle is found in the common life the Holy Spirit produces.

When the Spirit came upon the disciples and they spoke in other tongues, the people who witnessed these ecstatic manifestations questioned them. Some thought the apostles were drunk. Peter gave a sermon explaining how these events were the fulfillment of prophecy from Joel that God would pour out the Holy Spirit on all flesh (Acts 2:17). In response to Peter's sermon, many people are converted. They came together and formed a common life.

> Awe came upon everyone, because many wonders and signs were being done by the apostles. All who believed were together and

had all things in common; they would sell their possessions and goods and distribute the proceeds to all, as any had need. Day by day, as they spent much time together in the temple, they broke bread at home and ate their food with glad and generous hearts, praising God and having the goodwill of all the people. And day by day the Lord added to their number those who were being saved. (Acts 2:43–47)

So what does the Holy Spirit do? The Spirit makes possible the witness of the church by creating a common life. This common life should have a social and economic manifestation, but a unity of doctrine, ritual, and discipline also characterizes it. To resist this unity is to resist the Holy Spirit. The Spirit is the unity between Father and Son. When the Spirit constitutes the church, it will participate in this unity. As St. Basil recognized, through the Spirit "the Church is set in order." The church is constituted and ordered through the gifts of the Holy Spirit.[5] Yves Congar, an important Catholic theologian who wrote on the Holy Spirit, made four key points about the relationship between the Spirit and the church.

1. The church is made by the Spirit.

2. The Spirit is the principle of communion.

3. The Spirit is the principle of catholicity.

4. The Spirit keeps the church apostolic.[6]

When we discuss the teachings on the church, we will return to these four points. They are known as the "four marks" of the church; it is holy, one, catholic, and apostolic.

It is the Holy Spirit who inspires Scripture and allows us to receive it as we should. Article four of our Confession of Faith explicitly states this. We turn next to Holy Scripture.

---

5. St. Basil, *On the Holy Spirit*, 65.

6. See vol. 2 of Congar's *I Believe in the Holy Spirit*.

Questions for Consideration:

1. Who is the Holy Spirit?

2. What is the importance of *lex orandi, lex credendi*?

3. What are the implications of denying the divinity of the Holy Spirit?

4. How do you understand the Holy Spirit?

5. What does it mean to say that the Holy Spirit is both the object of prayer and the means of prayer?

6. What are the two common errors in speaking about the Holy Spirit?

7. What does the Holy Spirit do?

8. What are some of the key passages of Scripture that help us understand the Spirit?

9. What kind of community does the Spirit create? What are the political and economic implications of the Spirit's activity in the church?

10. What are the four key points we need to keep in mind about the relationship between the Spirit and the church?

five

Holy Scripture

Confession of Faith: Article IV: **The Holy Bible**

We believe the Holy Bible, Old and New Testaments, reveals the Word of God so far as it is necessary for our salvation. It is to be received through the Holy Spirit as the true rule and guide for faith and practice. Whatever is not revealed in or established by the Holy Scriptures is not to be made an article of faith nor is it to be taught as essential to salvation.

Articles of Religion: Article V: **Of the Sufficiency of the Holy Scriptures for Salvation**

The Holy Scripture containeth all things necessary to salvation; so that whatsoever is not read therein, nor may be proved thereby, is not to be required of any man that it should be believed as an article of faith, or be thought requisite or necessary to salvation. In the name of the Holy Scripture we do understand those canonical books of the Old and New Testament of whose authority was never any doubt in the church. The names of the canonical books are: Genesis, Exodus, Leviticus, Numbers, Deuteronomy, Joshua, Judges, Ruth, The First Book of Samuel, The Second Book of Samuel, The First Book of Kings, The Second Book of Kings, The First Book of Chronicles, The Second Book of Chronicles, The Book of Ezra, The Book of Nehemiah, The Book of Esther, The Book of Job, The Psalms, The Proverbs, Ecclesiastes or the Preacher, Cantica or Songs of Solomon, Four Prophets the Greater, Twelve Prophets the Less. All the books of the New Testament, as they are commonly received, we do receive and account canonical.

We cannot adequately discuss Holy Scripture without understanding who the Holy Spirit is, and what the Holy Spirit does. As we mentioned above, if we hear the Word of God in Scripture, this is a result not of our own natural intelligence, but of the gift of God's Spirit poured out upon the church at Pentecost. For this reason, before we read Scripture, we pray for illumination by the Spirit. The standard prayer is, "Open our hearts and minds by the power of your Holy Spirit, that as the Scriptures are read and your Word proclaimed, we may hear with joy what you say to us today." This lets us know something about Holy Scripture; it is not just black marks on white paper. It is a living, dynamic book that comes to life best when it is read and interpreted within the life of the church. The book itself is not the "authority," which is the living Triune God who makes this book His own speech to us. Therefore, the Bible is not a book that each individual should interpret for him or herself. Our Confession begins with the important statement, "*We* believe in the Holy Bible . . ." It is not "I," but "we." In fact, many errors arise in the life of the church when individuals claim that their own peculiar reading of the Bible matters more than the received, collective wisdom of the church.

We Believe the Holy Bible . . .

The Bible is first and foremost the book of the church. The church gave the Bible its "canonical" form, and yet the Bible also makes the church what it is. Or to put this more succinctly, the church "made" the Bible, even though the Bible makes the church. This is why our fifth Article of Religion states that we accept the "canonical books" as they are "commonly received." This should remind us that the United Methodist Church does not think of itself as unique, but takes its place with all other churches under the authority of Holy Scripture, which is what the term "canonical" means. This term comes from the Greek word *kanōn*. It literally meant a straight rule that was used for construction—what we would now call a level. To use it for Scripture is to use it metaphorically. It is a rule that has a common authority behind it. For example, that we should drive our cars only on a certain side of the road or else suffer the consequences can be understood as a "canon." It is received, common wisdom that now has the backing of authority. This rule is then "canonical": it characterizes (or should) our life together on the roads. Likewise, the books of the Bible that are canonical are those the church commonly accepted as authoritative that then make possible our common life. Many other books and letters from the apostolic age are known to us, as they were known to the followers of Jesus in those days. For instance, the Gospel of Judas was known to the early church father Irenaeus, and he rejected it. It became noncanonical, as did the Gospel of Thomas and the Gospel of Barnabas. The early church found these books to be inadequate in telling the Christian story. Notice that none of these books is listed in the recognized canonical list in our fifth Article of Religion. Therefore, they cannot be used in church. Anyone who would substitute these noncanonical books for a canonical reading in worship would violate his or her ordination or membership vows. They would place their own private judgment above that of the common consensus of the church's apostolicity, catholicity, and unity (more on that below). Wesleyans adhere to the traditional canonical texts, and individuals cannot decide for themselves to substitute other texts. The canonical texts are the only ones that should be read and given authority in our church's life. Yet we must remember that a book is not finally what has authority, but God. Only inasmuch as God "authorizes" Scripture is it an authority for us.

We Believe the Holy Bible, Old and New Testaments . . .

How should we refer to the two testaments that make up the Holy Bible? They are traditionally known as the Old and New Testaments. These terms have theological reasons behind them. Jesus presents his life and work as the fulfillment of the Jewish Scriptures. Jesus states,

> Do not think that I have come to abolish the law or the prophets;
> I have come not to abolish but to fulfill. For truly I tell you, until
> heaven and earth pass away, not one letter, not one stroke of a let-
> ter, will pass from the law until all is accomplished. (Matt 5:17–18)

In these words, Jesus attests that the Jewish Scriptures remain in effect; he has not come to do away with them, and at the same time, he fulfills them. This helps us understand why Christians now refer to the Jewish Scriptures as the Old Testament. We do not mean by this that the old is somehow worn out or bad and therefore replaced by the new. Only in a culture such as ours, obsessed with always looking youthful, could *old* be construed as "worn out" or "bad." *Old* here has two functions. First, it reminds us that without the stories of Israel, we would not know who Jesus is. If we did not know God's Name as revealed in Exodus 3, we would never have known that Jesus bears the Name. For this reason, we have an assigned reading from the Old Testament every Sunday, and it is usually read first. The Old Testament is the necessary precondition for understanding the New. We must read the New Testament based on the foundation of the Old. It has not been abolished. One of the great errors in the church occurred when some people wanted to do away with the Old Testament because they thought it bore witness to a god other than the God Christians worship. This was called the Marcionite heresy and was rejected by the early church. The Jewish Scriptures are also Christian Scripture, which is to say that the Old Testament is as much Christian Scripture as is the New.

Second, the term *old* reminds us that Jesus fulfills the Jewish Scripture. He is the Messiah, and we are no longer waiting for his advent—although we are waiting for his return. This is an important disposition we share with Jews. In this sense, members of both faiths are still waiting for the Messiah. Christians think he has already been here; Jews think he has not. A common saying in Christian and Jewish relations is that this disagreement cannot be resolved until the Messiah (finally) comes. When he comes, we will ask him, "Have you been here before?" If he says yes, Christians will be right. If no, Jews will be right. Either way, we both trust that the Messiah is merciful. Because Jesus fulfills the law and the prophets, he is the New that helps make sense of their older witness. Christians must read the Old Testament based on its foundation in Jesus and the New Testament. This is why we also always have a reading from the New Testament, and especially the Gospels, in our worship. Some people no longer want to use the terms *Old Testament* and *New Testament*. They substitute terms such as *Hebrew Scriptures* or *Jewish Scriptures* for *Old Testament*, and *Christian Scriptures* for *New Testament*. Or sometimes they use the words *first* and *second* to refer to the testaments. These are often thought to be more neutral terms that will not unnecessarily cause offense to our Jewish neighbors. But when we realize that the terms *old* and *new* make a statement about who Jesus is for Christians, then we

recognize that these new terms are not neutral; rather they often have behind them an unwillingness to confess that Jesus has the uniqueness our
church's articles claim for him. We must first reject that he is the "eternal
Word made flesh" before we can accept the alternative language.

We Believe the Holy Bible, Old and New Testaments, Reveals the Word of God . . .

Our Confession states that the Word of God, who is Jesus, is found in
both testaments. The Triune God speaks throughout the Scripture. This
never meant that every word is somehow a command that should be emulated. Scripture contains statements that we rightly find problematic. It
advocates stoning children for disrespect. We have stories of incredible
violence—including the command to destroy all persons and their possessions from a conquered people (Lev 27:29; Josh 6:17). The Levitical
priesthood begins through fratricide (Exod 32:25–27). The judge Jepthah
sacrifices his daughter to keep a vow (Judg 11:34–40). The Psalms speak
favorably of dashing babies against rocks (Ps 137:9). In the New Testament,
women are told to be silent in the church, and wives are told to obey their
husbands and slaves their masters. Many people rightly ask, how do such
stories reveal the Word of God?

We cannot, and should not, excise these stories from the Scriptures.
They too are the "Word of God." Because the Holy Spirit is present in the
writing and transmission of the texts and in their ongoing vitality in the
life of the church, we must always recognize that God is not somehow
"hidden" in the text, as if we must be detectives searching for a God who
intentionally evades us. Nonetheless, the meaning of Scripture is not as
obvious as some have thought. This is not because God is hidden, but
because God is revealed! As St. Anselm put it, God is that splendor of
luminosity who only appears hidden because He is the perfected light of
holiness that blinds our feeble intellects. If Scripture appears contradictory or even morally questionable, we must not try to stand over and
against it in order to judge it, but we must stand within and beneath it and
read it against our own sinful intellects. Without a doubt, when we look
at these and other passages, exactly how they are the Word of God does
not always come readily into focus. Several things must be kept in mind in

hearing God's Word in and through such texts. First, no single text should be isolated from its context both within a particular narrative and within the biblical story as a whole. Let me give an example of what I mean. We often hear Scripture derided as evil because it legitimated slavery. We could certainly find texts that lend support to such a claim, as did those who owned and trafficked in slaves. Such uses we now rightly judge as not only improper but downright vicious. Scripture cannot legitimate slavery, because slavery is evil and evil is "lack," is absence, which God who is cannot possess. Oliver O'Donovan, a careful reader of Scripture, shows how Paul could not finally advocate slavery because he graciously transforms the master-slave relationship by referring to both as "brothers." How can brothers finally own one another? Likewise, how is it faithful to prohibit women from teaching, preaching, and presiding in the church on the basis of one text in Paul when other texts tell us that women led house churches and had great responsibility in Christ's mission? They were, after all, the first witnesses and proclaimers of the resurrection. If Mary had not said "yes," the incarnation would not have happened. She first made Jesus present in the world. How is that not a sacramental image?

Second, not every text is to be read in the same way. Not all commands have the same status, and both Jews and Christians recognize this by the way they reread the commandments in light of other commandments. A Jewish rabbi once told me that he was asked by a Christian where his congregation keeps the animals for sacrifice, as the Levitical law required. This Christian failed to see that Judaism, like Christianity, is not bound to a mindless obedience to biblical commands, but reads the commands within God's overarching, merciful and gracious covenant. No one follows, or has ever followed, all the rules laid out in the book of Leviticus. We even find corrections of Scripture in Scripture itself, such as when the Holy Spirit commands Peter to eat profane food that had earlier been deemed unclean (Acts 10:9–16). Third, we must remember that not everything in Scripture is a command to be obeyed or an example to emulate. If we find a command morally repugnant, it may very well be that this repugnance is a Spirit-led response that helps us understand God's Word in this passage. The story of Jepthah's daughter is not an example to be followed any more than is the fratricide in Exodus 32. These are stories that let us know something has gone horribly wrong, and we have not yet heard the definitive Word emanating from Scripture if our faith stops before such passages and finds solace. They are nonetheless the Word of God that must be heard.

Finally, we must recall that Scripture is to be read with a faith that seeks understanding. We reason about Scripture, which is a sign of our faith. For instance, even though Scripture tells us that Noah shut the doors to the ark and that God walked with Adam and Eve in the garden, this does not mean that any Jewish or Christian interpreter ever taught that God has a body with arms to shut doors and legs to walk in gardens. The first commandment teaches us that God is not a creature and thus cannot be such. Thus faith itself requires that we think and reason about what these stories might mean without assuming that they are to be taken just as they are without reasonable interpretation.

> We believe the Holy Bible, Old and New Testaments, reveals the Word of God, so far as it is necessary for our salvation. The Holy Scripture containeth all things necessary to salvation; so that whatsoever is not read therein, nor may be proved thereby, is not to be required of any man that it should be believed as an article of faith, or be thought requisite or necessary to salvation.

But what constitutes reasonable interpretation? How does faith seek reason in reading the Bible well? These questions can be ways we avoid hearing the Word of God revealed in Scripture in favor of our own peculiar words. No precise answer can be given to these questions. Yet we must avoid two things. First, we must avoid a "fideism" that rejects reason for faith and claims that the Bible must be taken as is without interpretation—as if that were possible. Second, we must avoid a "rationalism" that rejects faith and stands over and against the Scriptures, subjecting them to our categories without receiving them in faith.

A number of ways of interpreting the Scriptures have emerged in Christian history. The ancient church taught a fourfold interpretation of Scripture based on the allegorical, tropological (moral), anagogical (eschatological), and literal meanings. This fourfold method was related to the theological virtues of faith, hope, and charity. It was assumed that Scripture did not have a single meaning, but it had a meaning that would produce the virtue of faith. This was the allegorical meaning, which was related to the church's doctrinal confessions. It would also produce the virtue of charity, which was the "tropological" or moral meaning. And it would produce the virtue of hope, which was the "anagogical" or eschatological meaning. "Eschatology" is the teaching about God's ultimate triumph over evil and the restoration of things in God's image. The "literal" meaning should produce all these virtues. Because Paul taught us that these are the things that "remain"—faith, hope, and love—they were understood to be the ultimate meaning of Scripture. If reading Scripture produces vice rather than virtue, then we are not yet reading Scripture well.

In Protestant circles, the literal meaning of Scripture became the predominant meaning. Good reasons existed for this switch to the literal meaning. The fourfold interpretation, especially when it was not regulated by the church's confessions, could lead to some fanciful interpretation. It did not always seem to prevent the interpreter from finding in the Bible whatever he or she wanted to find. Thus traditions of interpretation developed that seemed unrelated to what the Scripture actually said. This is one reason why our Article states, "whatsoever is not read therein, nor may be proved thereby, is not to be required of any man that it should be believed as an article of faith, or be thought requisite or necessary to salvation." This reflects the Protestant commitment to the literal interpretation. In response to the Reformation, some Catholics argued for two sources of authority—Scripture and tradition—although this is an innovation within Catholicism, for prior to the Reformation, Catholicism had only one source: Scripture. Tradition was primarily the ongoing interpretation of Scripture and not a separate source. Protestants argued that the only source of authority is Scripture and it is to be primarily understood as literal. But what is meant by "literal" can easily be misleading. By "literal," the Protestant Reformers meant "the sense of the letter."[1] The sense of the letter may be metaphorical. Therefore the literal meaning could be metaphorical. This flies in the face of much modern interpretation, which distinguishes the literal from the metaphorical. Here the literal usually means that the words have a one-to-one correspondence to some historical referent. The metaphorical does not have such a historical reference but is a "surprising conjunction of terms." That God is love is literal; that

---

1. Wright, *The Last Word*, 73.

God is a lion is metaphorical. But as N. T. Wright notes, this is not what the Reformers meant by literal.

The literal sense actually means the sense of the letter, and if the letter—the actual words used by the original author or editors—is metaphorical, so be it. Thus, confusingly for us perhaps, the literal sense of Psalm 18:8, which speaks of smoke coming out of God's nostrils, is that, by this rich metaphor, the psalmist is evoking the active and terrifying indignation of the living God against those who oppress his people.[2]

In modern Protestant thought, the literal interpretation led to two kinds of interpretation, one known as inerrancy and the other as infallibilism. Strong inerrantists argue that the literal interpretation means that every word must have a one-to-one correspondence with a historical referent. Therefore, the creation story in Genesis 1 can only be interpreted in terms of a seven-day creation where what is meant by a "day" must be equivalent to what we mean today by a "day." Such creationist readings are difficult to sustain. The early church fathers and the Reformers did not mean this when they spoke of a literal interpretation. In fact, the second-century theologian Origen did not mean this, even though he would advocate inerrancy, as did John Wesley. Origen knew that Scripture could not mean this, for the creation story speaks of a day before God creates the sun and moon. Strong inerrantists are fundamentalists; they treat the Bible like a scientific textbook rather than the living Word of God. The United Methodist Articles of Religion do not support their reading of Scripture. Fundamentalism and the United Methodist tradition are at odds. But there are also "weak inerrantists," who allow for the kind of literal interpretation that N. T. Wright described above. They recognize the importance of genre, and thus they would see the book of Jonah as literally true, even though they have no commitment to large fishes swallowing up people and spitting them out unharmed on dry land. The literal truth of the book of Jonah is found in the wisdom it intends to teach and not in some scientific statement about the digestive system of large fishes.

Infallibilists distance themselves from inerrantists. Even though weak inerrantists allow for flexibility in interpreting Scripture, infallibilists find the term "inerrant" too loaded with a modern, scientific approach to the Bible. They argue that the Scriptures are "infallible" when it comes

2. Ibid.

to faith and morals, but not necessarily every statement on cosmology, history, science, anthropology, and so on. The United Methodist article on Scripture would allow for a weak inerrantist position as well as an infallibilist one. The latter seems closest to the statement in our article that Holy Scripture "reveals the Word of God, so far as it is necessary for our salvation." It does not reveal everything we need to know. We still need to learn from other books about science, politics, economics, and history. But when it comes to what we need to know for salvation, Holy Scripture reveals the Word of God without error.

Another form of literal interpretation is the modern scientific historical-critical method, which is the method of biblical interpretation that is almost exclusively taught in contemporary seminaries. In some versions, it supposedly approaches the Bible without any theological presuppositions, and only seeks to discover what the text meant to the original writers. Then it tries to make a leap from that original meaning to what it means for us to day. When it is thus understood, it is similar to fundamentalism in the way that it understands the literal meaning, except that the historical-critical method honors the findings of contemporary science more so than does fundamentalism. The historical-critical method has produced some important results in understanding the Bible as ancient literature, but it lacks the richness of more traditional, theological interpretations of the Bible.

> It is to be received through the Holy Spirit as the true rule and guide for faith and practice.

The Bible is more than ancient literature; it is "the true rule and guide for faith and practice." It is this only as it is "received through the Holy Spirit."

Questions for Consideration:

1. What is the connection between the Holy Spirit and the church?

2. What does it mean that the church made the Bible and the Bible makes the church?

3. What do we mean by "Old Testament" and "New Testament"?

4. What do we mean when we say that the Holy Bible reveals the Word of God?

5. What do we need to keep in mind when we read and interpret Scripture?

6. What constitutes reasonable interpretation?

7. What strengths do you see in the ancient way of interpreting the Scriptures?

8. What does "literal" mean? How is this a virtue? How is this a vice?

9. Where can a literal interpretation of Scripture lead with respect to modern ideas of inerrancy and infallibility?

10. What is the difference between a "weak inerrantist" and "strong inerrantist"?

11. What are the strengths and weaknesses of the historical-critical method?

12. What does it mean that the Scriptures are to be received through the Holy Spirit as the rule and guide for faith?

six

The Church

Confession of Faith: Article V: **The Church**

We believe the Christian Church is the community of all true believers under the Lordship of Christ. We believe it is one, holy, apostolic and catholic. It is the redemptive fellowship in which the Word of God is preached by men divinely called, and the sacraments are duly administered according to Christ's own appointment. Under the discipline of the Holy Spirit the Church exists for the maintenance of worship, the edification of believers and the redemption of the world.

Articles of Religion: Article XIII: **Of the Church**

The visible church of Christ is a congregation of faithful men in which the pure Word of God is preached, and the Sacraments duly administered according to Christ's ordinance, in all those things that of necessity are requisite to the same.

Articles of Religion: Article XXII: **Of the Rites and Ceremonies of the Church**

It is not necessary that rites and ceremonies should in all places be the same, or exactly alike; for they have always been different, and may be changed according to the diversity of countries, times and men's manners, so that nothing be ordained against God's Word. Whosoever, through his private judgment, willingly and purposely doth openly break the rites and ceremonies of the church to which he belongs, which are not repugnant to the Word of God, and are ordained and approved by common authority, ought to be rebuked openly, that others may fear to do the like, as one that offendeth against the common order of the church, and woundeth the consciences of weak brethren. Every particular church may ordain, change, or abolish rites and ceremonies so that all things may be done to edification.

Apart from the three Persons of the Trinity, the only other object of our belief in the Nicene Creed is the church—"we believe in one holy catholic and apostolic church." Our Confession of Faith and Articles of Religion follow closely the Nicene Creed by also making the church an object of our confession: "We believe the Christian Church is . . ." We make two claims about the church in our confession. First, "We believe the Christian Church is the community of all true believers under the Lordship of Christ." By this confession, we recognize that the true church is larger than the United Methodist Church. All "true believers" who are a "community under the Lordship of Christ" constitute the church. The church is not a collection of individuals, but a community. True belief cannot occur without participation in such a community, but the community cannot be the church if it does not place itself under the Lordship of Christ. To be subject to a community for the sake of community is no more redemptive than to be an individual standing alone. What makes the church is not the gathering of a community, but the gathering of a community that recognizes Christ as its head. If the bishop, a charismatic leader, a democratic process, a political interest, or any other such thing is the authority under which a community gathers rather than Christ, then it is not the church.

Second, "We believe the church is one holy catholic and apostolic." These are the four marks of the church that are found in the Nicene Creed. These two confessions mutually enrich each other. We understand what it means for the church to be one, holy, catholic, and apostolic when we see the church as a true community under the Lordship of Christ. Likewise we understand what it means for the church to be a true community under Christ's Lordship when we find in it the marks of unity, holiness, catholicity, and apostolicity. The church becomes this through the Holy Spirit; it cannot become this on its own. Yves Congar stated that the church is made by the Spirit, who is the principle of communion and catholicity and keeps the church apostolic. In other words, the Spirit's work is associated with the "four marks" of the church. The Spirit's presence makes it holy and in so doing "communicates" God's own presence to it. This "communication" produces a "communion" that makes it one. This unity exists in every time and place and thus is "catholic." But it also always connects the church to its originating mission and witness, which was and is the work of the apostles. We will examine all four marks.

Unity

The church is One because it is the body of Christ, and Christ's body cannot be divided. Jesus prayed that all his followers would be "completely one." He prayed,

> As you, Father, are in me and I am in you, may they also be in us, so that the world may believe that you have sent me. The glory that you have given me I have given them, so that they may be one, as we are one. I in them and you in me, that they may become completely one, so that the world may know that you have sent me and have loved them even as you have loved me. (John 17:21–23)

The unity of Christ's disciples is essential to his mission in the world; it is the reason he sends the Spirit on the church. If we are not one, then the world may not know that the Father sent the Son to love and redeem the world. Our unity reflects the life of the Trinity in the world. Paul also admonished us to have this kind of unity when he instructed us to "let the same mind be in you that was in Christ Jesus" (Phil 2:5). In the letter to the Ephesians, he stresses this unity:

> I, therefore, the prisoner in the lord, beg you to lead a life worthy of the calling to which you have been called, with all humility and gentleness, with patience, bearing with one another in love, making every effort to maintain the unity of the Spirit in the bond of peace. There is one body and one Spirit, just as you were called to the one hope of your calling, one Lord, one faith, one baptism, one God and Father of all, who is above all and through all and in all. (Eph 4:1–6)

If we are supposed to have this unity, how do we account for the scandalous fact of our divisions? After all, the church is divided among many competing churches, some of which do not recognize each other as legitimate expressions of Christianity. The history of the Wesleyan tradition has never been one of unity. First, the Church of England divided from the Roman Catholic Church. Then we broke off to form the Methodist Episcopal Church, which split over the question of slavery and then continued to divide until today we have so many different Wesleyan denominations that they are not easy to count. We have the African Methodist Episcopal Church, the United Methodist Church, the Nazarenes, the African Methodist Episcopal Church Zion, the Free Methdodists, the Christian Methodist Episcopal Church, the Wesleyans, the Church of God and more. The United Methodist Church is one of the more recent additions to the Wesleyan tradition. This is just to mention some of the divisions within the Wesleyan tradition, let alone the greater Protestant and Orthodox traditions. Given the history of division and conflict within the church, do we dare confess that the church is "one"?

This raises the question, What makes the church "one"? For Roman Catholics, the unity of the church is found in the bishop of Rome. To be in the unity of the church requires communion with him. The Anglican Church has four instruments of unity: the archbishop of Canterbury; the Lambeth Conference; the Anglican Consultative Council, a permanent consultative body; and the Primates' Meeting, which is the gathering of the archbishops from all of the Anglican provinces. Both the Catholic and the Anglican Church are global; they seek to bring together into communion people from every nation on the planet. "Free" churches do not always have this same global reach. Rather than seeking that kind of unity, they seek only a local unity based on a commonly shared faith that would include doctrine and discipline. The Wesleyan tradition contains elements of both a free church and a Catholic or Anglican one. For instance, consistent with the free church tradition, we state that the unity of the church is found in "a congregation of faithful men in which the pure Word of God is preached." Here the unity of the church is found in the faithfulness of the gathered community. This could appear to be more of an "internal" source of authority, which is to say that the unity is not found in some external instrument. It is not a matter of being in communion with a bishop from Rome or Canterbury, but in participating in the faithfulness of the local church. Yet unlike Baptist or other free church bodies, we do not think that each local church has autonomy to determine for itself what constitutes that faithfulness. Thus we also state that the church's unity is found where "the Sacraments [are] duly administered according to Christ's ordinance" and where "the Word of God is preached by men divinely called, and the sacraments are duly administered according to Christ's own appointment." This constitutes an "external" instrument of unity. How do we know where the Word of God is rightly preached and the sacraments "duly administered" by persons "divinely called"? Like the Anglican and Catholics, this is a matter of being in communion with one's local bishop, who lays hands on those ordained and thus tells them to "take authority" to preach the gospel and administrate the sacraments. Most Wesleyans also have a conference that sets the doctrine and discipline of the church by which we can identify what it means to be "divinely called." We trust that the Holy Spirit works through this conferencing to lead us to discern how we are to structure our common life. Conferencing finds its biblical precedence in what the early disciples did in Acts 15 when they gathered to discern how the new community was to live.

Only the General Conference speaks officially for the United Methodist Church. The bishops are supposed to "guard and preserve" the teaching of the church as it comes down to us in our doctrines and discipline. They are not allowed to innovate and teach their own idiosyncratic theology. Likewise, pastors in charge of local churches are bound by the "yoke of obedience" to teach what the doctrine and discipline of the church sets forth. They are not allowed to put forth their own individual opinions as church teaching. If they do, they violate their ordination vows. This is why we have "chargeable offenses" for violating the doctrine and discipline of the church. Ordination is a communal rite, not an individual right.

Holiness

The holiness of the church should not be confused with a claim that people in the church are always morally superior to those outside the church. We know this is not always true. The church is holy because the Holy Spirit calls it into existence, not because the people who gather are themselves naturally morally superior. Our Confession states, "Under the discipline of the Holy Spirit the church exists for the maintenance of worship, the edification of believers and the redemption of the world." The Spirit disciplines us so that we might "maintain worship," "edify believers" and thereby "redeem the world."

Maintenance of Worship

Holiness is inseparable from the proper worship of God. The Holy Spirit disciplines the church by leading it into proper worship. This is why the sacrament of initiation into the church is baptism. It reminds us that our own efforts to be holy always fail, and we must first have our will and our intellect transformed by the Spirit's power at baptism so that we might be holy as God intends. Baptism is a mini-exodus. Just as Israel left Egypt to travel with God in the desert to the promised land, so we are called out of sinfulness to sojourn with God to that holy city God prepares for us. It is the journey that makes us holy, not the power of our own will and intellect. This holiness comes as a gift and not an accomplishment. We must participate in the gift; we must receive it and continually act on it, making it our own. No one in the church has ever thought that the water of baptism was magical, as if someone could just throw the water on another who would then be suddenly and instantly transformed. Baptism, like the Eucharist, must be received by faith for it to be efficacious.

Faith is also a gift of the Holy Spirit that makes us holy, but it is not a gift that God forces upon us. We freely receive and act upon it. We must voluntarily enter into the journey of discipleship, but faith is given to anyone who asks. Thus, unlike certain Calvinist churches in which Jesus' death on the cross is not intended for all, in the Wesleyan tradition, as the Scripture clearly states, Jesus died for all. The Wesleyan hymn "Come, Sinners, to the Gospel Feast" sets this forth nicely:

> Come, sinners, to the gospel feast;
> let every soul be Jesus' guest.
> Ye need not one be left behind,
> for God hath bid all humankind.[1]

Christ's sacrifice on the cross is for everyone. God seeks to sanctify the world, and potentially every human creature, by inviting him or her to

---

1. *United Methodist Hymnal*, 339.

baptism and Eucharist whereby God makes us holy by allowing us to participate in God's own life. Our holiness, then, is a participated holiness. In the Methodist tradition, it is no sin to hope that all might be saved.

Baptism and Eucharist are connected. Baptism is the initiation into Christ's body, which should only be done once. Eucharist is the repeatable feast whereby we boldly commune with God because of what Christ has done for us. For this reason, the Eucharist presupposes the transformation that occurs at baptism. To teach that people can come to the Eucharist without baptism is to deny that our holiness is a participated holiness, and to assume that we can come to Jesus without the grace of baptism. It is to fall into the Pelagian heresy of thinking we have all that we need to live into God's holiness simply by being creatures. Baptism reminds us that we do not have what we need without first following Jesus through his death and resurrection. Through baptism we receive the grace that allows us to participate in the Eucharist. Frequent participation in the Eucharist strengthens and confirms the grace offered to us at baptism, a grace that must always be received by faith. The next lesson will discuss more fully what the Wesleyan tradition believes about Baptism and the Lord's Supper. The early Wesleyans were supposed to receive the Lord's Supper frequently; it is even in their general rules. This is a crucial reason why we ordain clergy. If they do not provide frequent celebrations of the Lord's Supper, the reason for ordination makes little sense.

Edification of Believers

The Wesleyan General Rules expect Methodists to attend regularly upon the Lord's Supper. This is not to be done as a mere ritual, but so that we might receive the grace to live a life of holiness. Mr. Wesley recognized that one of the problems in the church of his day was a "formality" to religion that did not lead to a proper edification of believers. In the preface to his published sermons, he explained that his work had two purposes, the first of which was "to guard those who are just setting their faces toward heaven . . . from formality, from mere outside religion, which has almost driven heart-religion out of the world." Formality occurs when we are more concerned with the "forms" by which we worship than we are with what those forms are supposed to accomplish in our lives. In other words, we say all the proper words and follow the correct procedures, have no effect. They do not make us more Christlike, more hc_, sought to guard the Methodist people against such a mere formality in our worship and common life, which occurs when institutional procedures become more central than the practices that lead to holiness.

The Methodist concern against formality never led Wesley or the Methodists to reject proper forms of worship as inconsequential to the religion of the heart. Rules and correct liturgical forms were not abandoned, but they were put in their proper place. This is captured in Wesley's second stated purpose for his work: "to warn those who know the religion of the heart, the faith which worketh by love, lest at any time they make void the law through faith, and so fall back into the snare of the devil."[2] In other words, one error in the life of the church is to have all the proper forms in our worship, doctrine, and discipline, but nothing more than these forms, which do not *do* anything; they do not produce the "religion of the heart." A second error is to think we can have the religion of the heart without the proper forms of worship, doctrine, and discipline. Although our church recognizes a proper diversity of such forms (see Article XXII above), we also confess that no one should take it upon him or herself to alter these forms solely based on her or his private judgment. For this reason, the articles state, "Whosoever, through his private judgment, willingly and purposely doth openly break the rites and ceremonies of the church to which he belongs, which are not repugnant to the Word of God, and are ordained and approved by common authority, ought to be rebuked openly, that others may fear to do the like, as one that offendeth against the common order of the church, and woundeth the consciences of weak brethren." We Methodists find the rites and ceremonies of our church to be so important that openly breaking them should issue in a rebuke, even if that rebuke must be given to a pastor, superintendent, or bishop. The rites and ceremonies belong to the whole church. When a pastor, superintendent, or bishop changes those rites and ceremonies because of her or his individual conscience, she or he violates the trust that the church places in her or him to guard and preserve the faith. The forms of our rules, worship, and doctrine do not guarantee holiness (the religion of the heart). But the latter does not cancel out those forms. They

2. Wesley, *Works*, 1:106.

are necessary if we are to have the proper edification of believers. What is this proper edification? It is to have our lives embody the life of blessedness or beatitude that Jesus pronounced in his Sermon on the Mount. This is what Wesley meant by the "religion of the heart," which is poverty of spirit, meekness, mourning, righteousness, mercifulness, purity of heart, peaceableness, and persecution for righteousness' sake. He did not teach that the "religion of the heart" was some inward experience of God that could only be known by an individual believer. The religion of the heart is a life lived in conformity with what Jesus pronounced as blessed in his Sermon on the Mount (Matt 5–7). The purpose of the church's discipline, doctrine, and worship is to cultivate this way of life, to "edify" believers into it. But we should never think of discipline, doctrine, and worship as a formal means to the religion of the heart that can be dispensed with once we think we have heart religion. We will return to these important themes in our ninth lesson on the Christian life.

Redemption of the World

The church is not an enclave that exists for its own sake; it is one of the forms of Christ's body, and Christ seeks to draw all people to him. Therefore the church exists for the sake of Christ's mission, which is nothing short of the redemption of the world. This is Christian hope. Lesson three discussed this in explaining the importance of Jesus' return. There we mentioned the passage of the final vision found in the book of Revelation, which stated, "And I saw no temple in the city, for its temple is the Lord God the Almighty and the Lamb. And the city has no need of sun or moon to shine upon it, for the glory of God is its light, and its lamp is the Lamb. By its light shall the nations walk; and the kings of the earth shall bring their glory into it, and its gates shall never be shut by day—and there shall be no night there; they shall bring into it the glory and the honor of the nations." Christian hope is that the nations of the world will learn to "walk" by the light of Christ, a light that he shines in the Sermon on the Mount.

Catholicity

The word *catholic* means "according to the whole." The church is a global reality; it cannot be turned into an individual, regional, or national institution. United Methodism, as well as other Wesleyan churches, like our parent Anglican Church, stand in both the Catholic and Reformed traditions. This creates tensions, as well as opportunities. Unlike some Reformed churches, we do not believe in the autonomy of the congregation. Congregations cannot decide for themselves on issues of doctrine, worship, or discipline. We are a "connectional" church, which means that all United Methodist Churches are bound together not only by bonds of affection, but also by a discipline and an episcopal structure. But the United Methodist Church is not—and has never claimed to be—*the* catholic Church, or even the sole Wesleyan church. We are one church who confesses faith in a larger catholic Church, even though we have not yet experienced the true unity of that catholic Church. We are committed to that genuine catholicity. Our brothers and sisters are all Christians throughout the world. Our loyalty to them must come even before our loyalty to other important associations such as the family, corporation, or nation.

Apostolic

The "apostolic" nature of the church arises from the fact that the apostles' witness to Christ, especially as it comes to us through Holy Scripture, gives the church its basic form. It does this primarily through the Bible. One of the most important signs of the church's "apostolicity" is that we read the canonical biblical texts each Sunday and find in them God's Word. The apostles had access to that Word in a way different from our own. They walked and talked with Jesus both before and after his resurrection. After the resurrection, their witness became the basis for the Gospels in the New Testament. Whenever we gather as church and listen to this witness, we affirm the church's "apostolic" character.

A division does occur over whether the Scriptures alone provide the basis for the apostolic character of the church. For Catholics and Anglicans, the historic succession of bishops, supposedly from Peter until today, also provides the basis for the apostolic nature of the church. Bishops in apostolic succession lay hands on all the ordained in those two churches, giving it the form of a catholic unity dating back to Peter himself. Methodists tend to find this to be a "formality" that does not guarantee the apostolic nature of the church. We tend to side with the Orthodox Church, which finds "apostolicity" to be less a historical succession and more an eschatological reality where the witness of the apostles surrounds the church when it gathers consistent with the apostolic witness.

Questions for Consideration:

1. What are the two claims we make about the church?

2. What makes the church?

3. What are the four marks of the church?

4. How is the Holy Spirit associated with the four marks of the church?

5. What is unity in the church? How do we account for it?

6. What is holiness?

7. How does the Holy Spirit work to discipline us?

8. What does it mean to say that our holiness is a "participated holiness"?

9. How do we deny our holiness when we teach people that they can come to the Eucharist without baptism?

10. What was John Wesley's concern about the formality of religion?

11. What is the error of the religion of the heart without proper form?

12. Religion of the heart is more than an inward experience—what does this mean?

13. What does "catholic" mean?

14. What does "apostolic" mean?

seven

The Sacraments

Articles of Religion: Article XVI: **Of the Sacraments**

Sacraments ordained of Christ are not only badges or tokens of Christian men's profession, but rather they are certain signs of grace, and God's good will toward us, by which he doth work invisibly in us, and doth not only quickly but also strengthen and confirm our faith in him. There are two sacraments ordained of Christ our Lord in the Gospels; that is to say, Baptism and the Supper of the Lord. ... The Sacraments were not ordained of Christ to be gazed upon, or to be carried about; but that we should duly use them. And in such only as worthily receive the same, they have a wholesome effect or operation; but they that receive them unworthily, purchase to themselves condemnation, as St. Paul saith.

Articles of Religion: **Article XVII: Of Baptism**

Baptism is not only a sign of profession and mark of difference whereby Christians are distinguished from others that are not baptized; but it is also a sign of regeneration or the new birth. The Baptism of young children is to be retained in the Church.

Articles of Religion: **Article XVIII: Of the Lord's Supper**

The Supper of the Lord is not only a sign of the love that Christians ought to have among themselves one to another, but rather is a sacrament of our redemption by Christ's death; insomuch that, to such as rightly, worthily, and with faith receive the same, the bread which we break is a partaking of the body of Christ; and likewise the cup of blessing is a partaking of the blood of Christ.... The body of Christ is given, taken, and eaten in the Supper, only after a heavenly and spiritual manner. And the mean whereby the body of Christ is received and eaten in the Supper is faith.

Articles of Religion: **Article XIX: Of Both Kinds**

The cup of the Lord is not to be denied to the lay people; for both parts of the Lord's Supper, by Christ's ordinance and commandment, ought to be administered to all Christians alike.

Confession of Faith: **Article VI: The Sacraments**

We believe the Sacraments, ordained by Christ, are symbols and pledges of the Christian's profession and of God's love toward us. They are means of grace by which God works invisibly in us, quickening, strengthening and confirming our faith in him. Two sacraments are ordained by Christ our Lord, namely Baptism and the Lord's Supper. We believe Baptism signifies entrance into the household of faith, and is a symbol of repentance and inner cleansing from sin, a representation of the new birth in Christ Jesus and a mark of Christian discipleship. We believe children are under the atonement of Christ and as heirs of the Kingdom of God are acceptable subjects for Christian Baptism. Children of believing parents through Baptism become the special responsibility of the Church, and by profession of faith confirm their Baptism. We believe the Lord's Supper is a representation of our redemption, a memorial of the sufferings and death of Christ, and a token of love and union that Christians have with Christ and with one another. Those who rightly, worthily and in faith eat the broken bread and drink the blessed cup partake of the body and blood of Christ in a special manner until he comes.

Sacraments[1]

Both the Anglican Thirty-nine Articles and the United Methodist Twenty-five Articles bear the marks of the anti-Catholic protest that

---

1. Because the United Methodist Church has had so much confusion on the question of the sacraments, it commissioned two important studies to help both the clergy and the laity understand our teachings. The commissioned study on baptism is called "By Water and the Spirit," and the one on the Eucharist is called "This Holy Mystery." These texts should be consulted for a fuller understanding of the United Methodist position on the sacraments.

characterized the Anglican and Methodist Churches when these articles were formulated. We follow Martin Luther in rejecting five of the seven sacraments of the Catholics because no ordination for them can be found in Holy Scripture. This rejection relates back to the claim in Article IV of our Confession of Faith that "whatever is not revealed in or established by the Holy Scriptures is not to be made an article of faith nor is it to be taught as essential to salvation." Because these five are not found in Scripture, they were rejected. The five that were rejected are confirmation, penance, orders, matrimony, and extreme unction. We do all five of these practices, but we do not call them sacraments on their own. Confirmation and penance are now related to the sacrament of baptism. They take their meaning and significance from it. Marriage and ordination are not viewed as two different sacraments between which one chooses, and Methodists do not practice extreme unction, or last rites, although we do have a service for healing and forgiveness when death is impending.

Holy Eucharist

We also reject "transubstantiation," and in so doing are heirs of Luther, who taught that this doctrine had more to do with Aristotle than Holy Scripture. Transubstantiation is a Catholic teaching as to how the bread and wine become the body and blood of Christ. It is based on Aristotle's teaching that things are made up of substance and accidents. The substance constitutes what the thing is, and the accidents explain how it exists. Accidents can vary while the substance stays the same. Thus a chair will be a chair whether it is red, green, or blue, whether it has four legs or no legs or is of various heights. Aristotle did not teach that substances can change; bread will remain bread even though its accidents change, that is, though it has different colors, sizes, textures, and so on. The Catholic appropriation of Aristotle turned him on his head. It taught that it is possible for substance to change (*trans*-substantiation) even while accidents remain the same. The bread and wine of the Eucharist are no longer bread and wine, but they become body and blood. Christ's body is the true substance of the eucharistic meal. It is not always obvious that the Reformers understood what the Catholics were teaching. Likewise, the Catholic

Counter-Reformation against the Protestants did not always understand their positions well.

Many responses to Catholic transubstantiation were present during the Reformation. Lutheranism is often said to teach something called "consubstantiation" where the bread and wine remain bread and wine at the same time that they are the body and blood of Christ. (Luther, however, did not use this term.) At the other extreme of Catholicism is the teaching found by Zwingli and the more radical elements of the Reformation. For them, Christ's body is not really present in the Eucharist; it always remains in heaven (something John Calvin also taught), so that the bread and wine remain bread and wine and are only a "memorial meal" that functions more as a symbol than a real presence of Christ (something Calvin did not teach). Wesleyanism rejects both Catholic transubstantiation as an explanation as to how the bread and wine are changed and the Zwinglian view that nothing happens to the bread and wine because they are only symbols. In fact, Methodism affirms "real presence." We teach that "to such as rightly, worthily, and with faith receive the same, the bread which we break is a partaking of the body of Christ; and likewise the cup of blessing is a partaking of the blood of Christ." This is a real participation and not a mere memorial meal. This puts us on the Catholic side of the Catholic–Protestant divide. Many Catholics today argue that Christ's real presence in the elements is the important judgment we must make about what occurs in the sacrament, and transubstantiation is the conceptual apparatus that tries to explain it. We Methodists can reject that conceptual apparatus—as we do in our doctrines—and still agree with Catholics, Anglicans, and the Orthodox that Christ is really present in the sacrament.

The Wesleyan theology of the sacraments can be found most fully in Wesleyan hymns. Take, for example, the important hymn "Come, Sinners, to the Gospel Feast."[2]

> Come and partake the gospel feast,
> be saved from sin, in Jesus rest;
> O taste the goodness of our God,
> and eat his flesh and drink his blood.

---

2. *United Methodist Hymnal*, 616.

See him set forth before your eyes;
behold the bleeding sacrifice;
his offered love make haste to embrace,
and freely now be saved by grace.

This is not a hymn Zwingli could sing! It assumes that something actually occurs in the sacraments. Jesus is "set forth before our eyes" and we "eat his flesh and drink his blood." This requires faith, for of course what we naturally see set forth before our eyes and what we taste and drink appears to be nothing but bread and wine (or, unfortunately in our case, grape juice). Our intellect and our will cannot make it more than this. But the gift of faith allows us to see the miracle God works in our worship, a miracle similar to that of the incarnation. God becomes present in concrete, material existence so that we can participate in God's life.

Baptism

We find a similar understanding of baptism in our church. It is a material reality that effects a difference in the Christian's life. It is not only a symbol or sign of something that happened prior to the act itself; it brings with it "regeneration." Thus our article on baptism states, "Baptism is not only a sign of profession and mark of difference whereby Christians are distinguished from others that are not baptized; but it is also a sign of regeneration or the new birth." This qualifies, although it does not completely reject, two understandings of baptism. In the first, baptism is nothing more than the confirmation of a profession of faith. If it were this, then baptism would not be necessary for the life of the church. All that would really matter would be a person's "profession." This is not to suggest that a person's "profession" is immaterial to baptism; it matters. But it alone does not make the baptism, for if it did, baptism would depend solely upon the person and not upon God's prior action. Second, our understanding of baptism rejects the claim that its purpose is only to distinguish us from others as members of a holy community. Of course, baptism is this as well. Every baptism is a mini-exodus in which we are called to leave the "Egypt" that is our slavery to sin, pass through the waters, and then journey with God toward that Holy City that we await, where creation will be restored. Baptism marks us for that journey. It is why baptism is necessary for our participation in the Eucharist. If we do not first leave our "Egypt" and pass through the waters, we cannot faithfully receive the sustaining "manna" that guides us to God's Holy City. Jesus made this journey through his death and resurrection. Our baptism then is not only a participation in Israel's exodus, but also in Jesus' fulfillment of that exodus in his death and resurrection.

For Wesleyans, baptism is more than a person's profession and more than a distinguishing mark. It is also "regeneration." Baptism accomplishes something in the life of its recipient. It brings with it the "new birth." Every baptism is a participation in the life, death, and resurrection of Christ such that his work comes before the believer's profession or the church's call to be a gathered, holy community. This is why, when Karl Barth was asked, "When were you saved?" he responded, "33 AD." Jesus' mission on the cross has validity for each of God's creatures. It is what regenerates.

Validity and Efficacy of Sacraments

This of course does not mean that the human response is immaterial. Baptismal water does not save on its own; if it did, we could just throw holy water on unsuspecting people and thereby increase church membership. Likewise, we do not literally eat God such that we could give consecrated bread to people, have them eat it and thereby make them unwitting Christians. Although both baptism and Eucharist are concrete material realities, they do not work automatically like an automobile or a plane. When you get into one of those machines, it takes you to your destination irrespective of your faith in its efficacy. Baptism and Eucharist are not "machines" that cause a similar effect. When they are properly done, they are "valid" irrespective of the worthiness of the minister and congregation who preside over and witness to the sacrament, and irrespective of the worthiness of the recipient. But this does not make the sacrament efficacious. For it to be efficacious, it must be received by faith. For this reason our Article XVIII states, "The body of Christ is given, taken, and eaten in the Supper, only after a heavenly and spiritual manner. And the mean whereby the body of Christ is received and eaten in the Supper is faith." For baptism and Eucharist to accomplish their purposes in the world, it must be received in faith. If it is not, it will still be valid, but it will not be efficacious.

The distinction between the sacraments' validity and efficaciousness helps us understand statements in our Confession such as, "The Sacraments were not ordained of Christ to be gazed upon, or to be carried about; but that we should duly use them. And in such only as worthily receive the same, they have a wholesome effect or operation; but they that receive them unworthily, purchase to themselves condemnation, as St. Paul saith." The sacraments are not efficacious if they are simply part of some grand liturgical show and never received by faith. They are to be used for our sanctification; they are means, not ends. If we do not use them by receiving them with faith, then they can become dangerous, for they are still valid. They are offered to us, but without faith the offer is rejected. The result is that they can then condemn rather than sanctify. We become insensitive to the Spirit's presence, and rather than the sacraments drawing us into the life of God, they become an inoculation against it.

Communion of Saints and "Open" Communion

The regeneration that baptism brings, and the grace the Eucharist offers, is not only that of the individual believer, but also that of the whole communion of believers. The Eucharist is an "eschatological" meal. God intends to befriend us in the most intimate manner, and this occurs when we gather at table together. To eat with God is our hope. This has ancient biblical precedence. When God made the covenant with Israel, God summoned Moses, Aaron, Nadab, Abihu, and seventy elders to God's holy mountain. Scripture then recounts an odd story. It says,

> They saw the God of Israel. Under his feet there was something like a pavement of sapphire stone, like the very heaven for clearness. God did not lay his hand on the chief men of the people of Israel; also they beheld God, and they ate and drank. (Exod 24:9–11)

Likewise Jesus instituted the most sacred of meals at the Last Supper before he entered into his ultimate act of obedience through his betrayal, arrest, and crucifixion. He told us that he would not eat this meal again until he shared it with us. Nevertheless, he commanded us to do it "in remembrance of him." This is our "communion." It connects us to all Christians:

those who have come before us, those separated from us at present, and those who will come after us. We call this "the communion of saints." Our belief in it can be found both in the Nicene Creed and in our Confession of Faith. We confess, "We believe the Lord's Supper is a representation of our redemption, a memorial of the sufferings and death of Christ, and a token of love and union which Christians have with Christ and with one another." The Eucharist unites us first to Christ and then, through him, with all others who are thus united.

A great deal of debate today rages over the question of "open communion." This is a slippery phrase of recent origin. One cannot find it in Christian theologians prior to the 1970s. It cannot be found in Wesley. Open communion could mean that we as United Methodists honor all other church's baptisms. Closed communions are those that only allow people who are members of those communions, baptized into them, to come forward and receive the Eucharist. The various branches of the Christian tradition that merged to make up the United Methodist tradition never practiced that kind of closed communion. We are an ecumenical movement that honors all valid baptisms and invites all the baptized to share with us in "this holy mystery."

Recently, church leaders and theologians have begun to call for a different understanding of open communion, one that means that baptism is not a prerequisite for the Eucharist. Some refer to Mr. Wesley's statement that the Eucharist can be a "converting ordinance" to defend this innovation. Some people are so moved by the Spirit's presence in the Eucharist that they get converted through it. Therefore, some inquire, should we not allow for the possibility that an unbaptized person might come to faith through the Eucharist? Others argue that just as Jesus never asked anyone to change before he engaged in table fellowship with them, but welcomed all to the table, so we should follow his pattern. Baptism as a prerequisite for table fellowship seems to run counter to Jesus' generosity.

While we should allow for the exceptional circumstance when someone comes forward to receive the Eucharist as an act of conversion, we should not separate this desire from baptism. In fact, such an act is also at the same time a "desire for baptism." If people come forward and receive, and we discover that they have not been baptized (the eucharistic table is not the place or time to ask!), then they should be prepared for baptism.

Their participation in the Eucharist can be understood out of their desire for baptism. God works in mysterious ways, and sometimes with God causes come after effects.

The assumption that baptism is not necessary for the Eucharist because of Jesus' openness and inclusivity works against the whole narrative of Jesus' life as portrayed in the Scriptures. God's love for us in Christ cost God; it is a "costly" and not a "cheap" grace. Jesus said that if anyone wants to follow him, she must do so even to and through the cross. Baptism is where we begin this. Jesus never said that "you are accepted" irrespective of your willingness to enter into this task of discipleship. This would be to take God's ultimate act in Christ and turn it into "cheap" grace. If our lives could be transformed so easily, then they would be transformed simply by an act of divine power against us. We would not need Jesus' work on our behalf. If "open communion" is understood as a rejection of baptism as its prerequisite, then it is a form of Pelagianism where we assume that simply by virtue of our creation we have all that we need to stand before God. Our nature alone suffices; it does not require rebirth. For this reason, such an understanding of "open communion" works against the heart of our doctrines. It renders the sacraments irrelevant and makes Jesus superfluous to the Christian life.

Questions for Consideration:

1. What scriptural reasons do Wesleyan Christians have for practicing two sacraments?

2. What is the definition of *sacrament*?

3. What are the different understandings of the sacraments?

4. What is the role of faith in receiving the sacraments?

5. What is the connection between the role of the Holy Spirit and the sacraments?

6. What is baptism? What is the Eucharist?

7. What other names might we use to refer to the Eucharist? What do these names mean?

8. What makes the sacraments "efficacious"?

9. What are some common misperceptions about the sacraments?

10. How is "open communion" a form of Pelagianism? What is Pelagianism?

11. What are the standard practices of Holy Communion in your church?

eight

Justification and Sanctification

Articles of Religion: Article VII: **Of Original or Birth Sin**

Original sin standeth not in the following of Adam (as the Pelagians do vainly talk), but it is the corruption of the nature of every man, that naturally is engendered of the offspring of Adam, whereby man is very far gone from original righteousness, and of his own nature inclined to evil, and that continually.

Articles of Religion: Article VIII: **Of Free Will**

The condition of man after the fall of Adam is such that he cannot turn and prepare himself, by his own natural strength and works, to faith, and calling upon God; wherefore we have no power to do good works, pleasant and acceptable to God, without the grace of God by Christ preventing us, that we may have a good will, and working with us, when we have that good will.

Articles of Religion: Article IX: **Of the Justification of Man**

We are accounted righteous before God only for the merit of our Lord and Saviour Jesus Christ, by faith, and not for our own works or deservings. Wherefore, that we are justified by faith, only, is a most wholesome doctrine, and very full of comfort.

Articles of Religion: **Of Sanctification**

Sanctification is that renewal of our fallen nature by the Holy Ghost, received through faith in Jesus Christ, whose blood of atonement cleanseth from all sin;

whereby we are not only delivered from the guilt of sin, but are washed from its pollution, saved from its power, and are enabled, through grace, to love God with all our hearts and to walk in his holy commandments blameless.

Confession of Faith: Article VIII: **Reconciliation through Christ**

We believe God was in Christ reconciling the world to himself. The offering Christ freely made on the cross is the perfect and sufficient sacrifice for the sins of the whole world, redeeming man from all sin, so that no other satisfaction is required.

Confession of Faith: Article IX: **Justification and Regeneration**

We believe we are never accounted righteous before God through our works or merit, but that penitent sinners are justified or accounted righteous before God only by faith in our Lord Jesus Christ. We believe regeneration is the renewal of man in righteousness through Jesus Christ, by the power of the Holy Spirit, whereby we are made partakers of the divine nature and experience newness of life. By this new birth the believer becomes reconciled to God and is enabled to serve him with the will and the affections. We believe, although we have experienced regeneration, it is possible to depart from grace and fall into sin; and we may even then, by the grace of God, be renewed in righteousness.

Confession of Faith: Article XI: **Sanctification and Christian Perfection**

We believe sanctification is the work of God's grace through the Word and the Spirit, by which those who have been born again are cleansed from sin in their thoughts, words and acts, and are enabled to live in accordance with God's will, and to strive for holiness without which no one will see the Lord. Entire sanctification is a state of perfect love, righteousness and true holiness which every regenerate believer may obtain by being delivered from the power of sin, by loving God with all the heart, soul, mind and strength, and by loving one's neighbor as one's self. Through faith in Jesus Christ this gracious gift may be received in this life both gradually and instantaneously, and should be sought earnestly by every child of God. We believe this experience does not deliver us from the infirmities, ignorance, and mistakes common to man, nor from the possibilities of further sin. The Christian must continue on guard against spiritual pride and seek to gain victory over every temptation to sin. He must respond wholly to the will of God so that sin will lose its power over him; and the world, the flesh, and the devil are put under his feet. Thus he rules over these enemies with watchfulness through the power of the Holy Spirit.

A Wesleyan understanding of justification and sanctification stands not only in the Protestant but also in the Catholic tradition. This is why any adequate commentary on our Articles of Religion and Confession of Faith must be ecumenical in spirit. If we fail to see how we inherit both a Protestant and a Catholic understanding and practice of the faith, we will fail to understand well our Christian inheritance. This ecumenical spirit also brings with it tensions that are more like a task for us to work through than a completed state of doctrine.

Justification by Faith Alone

That our understanding of justification stands firmly in the Protestant tradition is not surprising. Our Confession states, "We believe we are never accounted righteous before God through our works or merit, but that penitent sinners are justified or accounted righteous before God only by faith in our Lord Jesus Christ." Likewise our articles affirm, "We are accounted righteous before God only for the merit of our Lord and Saviour Jesus Christ, by faith, and not for our own works or deservings." Notice that both these statements refer to "merit." The first states that we are "accounted" (not made) righteous not because of our own "works or merit," but "only by faith in our Lord Jesus Christ." The second empha-sizes that only the "merit" of Jesus allows us to be "accounted righteous." This emphasis on Christ's merit alone as well as the renunciation of our own merits is an anti-Catholic theme in our doctrine; it is thoroughly Protestant and indebted to Martin Luther. It is the Protestant theme of justification by faith alone.

Luther challenged the doctrine of merit in the Roman Catholic Church. He opposed John Tetzel, who preached indulgences, which as-sumed that certain works of ours could merit God's approval; they could even bring forgiveness to others. Tetzel supposedly stated, "When a coin in a coffer rings, a soul from purgatory springs." In other words, a donation to the church could produce merit that would not only forgive one's own sins, but also that of those in purgatory. Luther objected that this allowed for our merits to redeem rather than Christ's merit alone. Luther recognized that Christians were required to keep the commandments in order to be accounted righteous before God, but he thought this was impossible; even if we kept the law externally, even if we never violated the letter of the law, we still failed to keep it internally. We failed to keep the spirit of the law, and for Luther the law must be kept not only externally but also spiritually. This is our problem; we are required to keep the commandments but we cannot. Thus we cannot be justified; we cannot be accounted righteous before God.

Luther found the answer to our dilemma in Paul's letter to the Romans:

> Therefore, since we are justified by faith, we have peace with God through our Lord Jesus Christ. Through him we have obtained access to this grace in which we stand, and we rejoice in our hope of sharing the glory of God. (Rom 5:1–2)

In his preface to his commentary on Romans, Luther concluded:

> We reach the conclusion that faith alone justifies us and fulfills the law; and this because faith brings us the spirit gained by the merits of Christ. The spirit, in turn, gives us the happiness and freedom at which the law aims; and this shows that good works really proceed from faith. That is Paul's meaning in chapter 3 [v. 31] when, after having condemned the works of the law, he sounds as if he had meant to abrogate the law by faith; but says that on the contrary we confirm the law through faith, i.e. we fulfill it by faith.[1]

John Wesley's "heart-warming" experience occurred when he heard a reading from Luther's preface to the Romans. Although Wesley did not write either our articles or our Confession, we can readily see Luther's influence behind them: only the merits of Christ (and none of our own) allow us to be accounted righteous before God.

---

1. Luther, *Martin Luther: Selections from His Writings*, 22.

Sanctification

But are we to be more than "accounted righteous" before God? That we are accounted righteous before God because Jesus fulfills the Law and his righteousness is imputed to us forms the basis for the doctrine of justification. At its simplest, justification is what God does *for us* in Jesus Christ. But there is also something more to God's work of redemption. Sanctification is what God does *in us* through Jesus Christ in the Holy Spirit. We are not only *accounted* righteous, but we are *made* righteous. While the doctrine of justification assumes an "imputed" righteousness that is not our own, but rather is always "alien," the doctrine of sanctification assumes an "inherent" righteousness. The Holy Spirit does a work in us that makes us truly righteous. This is the basis for the Catholic doctrine of merit that many Protestants rejected, but not the Wesleyans. Central to this understanding of being made righteous is a passage in 2 Peter 1:4:

> Thus he has given us, through these things, his precious and very great promises, so that through them you may escape from the corruption that is in the world because of lust, and may become participants of the divine nature.

We find this passage cited in Article IX of our Confession of Faith: "We believe regeneration is the renewal of man in righteousness through Jesus Christ, by the power of the Holy Spirit, whereby we are made partakers of the divine nature and experience newness of life." Regeneration is the process not only of being *accounted* justified before God, but also of being *made* righteous. The latter is our sanctification, and in the Wesleyan tradition that sanctification can culminate in perfection. Wesleyan Christianity emphasizes this inherent righteousness perhaps more than any other movement within the Christian Church. It is why some Reformers accused Wesley and the Methodists of being too Catholic.

Perfection

The Methodists added a statement on sanctification that is not found in the thirty-nine Anglican articles; it states, "we are not only delivered from the guilt of sin." This tells us that Christ's work accomplishes something more than a mere alien righteousness. We are not only forgiven the guilt of sin, "but are washed from its pollution, saved from its power, and are enabled, through grace, to love God with all our hearts and to walk in his holy commandments blameless." Grace works a righteousness in us that allows us to keep the commandments without sin. This is the Wesleyan doctrine of perfection. We find it set forth in our Confession:

> We believe sanctification is the work of God's grace through the Word and the Spirit, by which those who have been born again are cleansed from sin in their thoughts, words and acts, and are enabled to live in accordance with God's will, and to strive for holiness without which no one will see the Lord. Entire sanctification is a state of perfect love, righteousness and true holiness which every regenerate believer may obtain by being delivered from the power of sin, by loving God with all the heart, soul, mind and strength, and by loving one's neighbor as one's self.

Several key points must be kept in mind if this doctrine is to be righly understood. First, sanctification and perfection are not moral achievements. The process of sanctification that can culminate in perfection is a gift that we receive from God, not a goal that we achieve through some proper method. If it were the latter, we Methodists would be guilty of the Pelagian heresy. Second, sanctification frees us from the power of sin so that we might live as God intends us to live. In other words, we can obey the Law. Law was important to Wesley and the early Wesleyans. It was why they set forth the "General Rules" as a form of discipline by which they established a common life. The third point is related to this second one. Making God's Name holy is done by loving God and loving one's neighbors. When Jesus summarized the whole law as loving God and neighbor, he was not inventing some new teaching but explaining the purpose of the law as God revealed it to Moses. The Law is not an end it itself, but directs us to the love of God and neighbor.

The Wesleyan doctrine of perfection can easily be misunderstood and lead to a presumptive self-righteousness that borders on the heresy of Pelagianism—we think we can obey God's laws by what we have in our nature, as it is, without the gift of a mediated grace. The Wesleyan emphasis on sanctification and perfection does not teach this. Perfection is a "work of God's grace through the Word and the Spirit." Our sanctification only occurs when the Triune life takes us up and allows us to participate in God's life.

Our doctrines repudiate Pelagianism. Article VII states that our sinful nature is not that we just follow Adam into sin (as if we could do otherwise); we are corrupted in our very nature. Our nature as it is cannot live as God requires, but graced nature can so live. Our doctrines teach that we can even walk "blamelessly" before God by performing good works. This is something we "obtain." It is a work of ours, without which we will not see God. How does this not approximate a Catholic doctrine of merit?

Many in Wesley's days feared that his work approximated the Catholic teaching. The Calvinist James Hervey asked, "But do not you believe inherent righteousness?" Wesley responded, "Yes, in its proper place; not as the ground of our acceptance with God, but as the fruit of it; not in the place of imputed righteousness, but as consequent upon it. That is I believe God implants righteousness in every one to whom he has imputed it."[2] Wesley worried that a doctrine of imputed righteousness alone could lead Christians to assume that they did not need to be righteous. For this reason he wrote an important sermon titled "The Lord our Righteousness," in which he said,

> In the meantime what we are afraid of is this: lest any should use the phrase, "the righteousness of Christ," or, "the righteousness of Christ is imputed to me," as a cover for his unrighteounsess . . . though a man be as far from the practice as from the tempers of a Christian, though he neither has the mind which was in Christ nor in any respect walks as he walked, yet he has armour of proof against all conviction in what he calls the "righteousness of Christ" . . . O warn them that if they remain unrighteous, the righteousness of Christ will profit them nothing.[3]

The United Methodist teaching is Protestant in that it teaches that we are justified by faith without any merits of our own. However, it is Catholic in that it insists that justification will produce fruits that enable the believer to fulfill the commandments.

---

2. Wesley, *Works*, 1:453.

3. Ibid., 1:462–63.

Protestants and Catholics Coming Together

The similarity between the Methodists and Catholics on justification and sanctification was acknowledged in 2006 when the World Methodist Council signed the "Joint Declaration on the Doctrine of Justification by the Lutheran World Federation and the Catholic Church." The Catholic Church and Lutheran World Federation affirmed this joint declaration on October 31, 1999. It is an amazing document that brings Protestants and Catholics closer together than they have ever been before. It renders obsolete some of the anti-Catholic language in our Articles and Confession, for now Catholics acknowledge that they agree with us and we agree with them that justification comes about solely from the merits of Christ. The joint declaration stated "that on the basis of their dialogue the subscribing Lutheran churches and the Roman Catholic Church are now able to articulate a common understanding of our justification by God's grace through faith in Christ." The heart of that common understanding is found in the statement, "Together we confess: By grace alone, in faith in Christ's saving work and not because of any merit on our part, we are accepted by God and receive the Holy Spirit, who renews our hearts while equipping and calling us to good works."

The relationship between a Catholic doctrine of merit and the connection between justification and sanctification was also explained in ways that Wesleyan Christians could recognize. "When Catholics affirm the 'meritorious' character of good works, they wish to say that, according to the biblical witness, a reward in heaven is promised to these works. Their intention is to emphasize the responsibility of persons for their actions, not to contest the character of those works as gifts, or far less to deny that justification always remains the unmerited gift of grace." If this is what Catholics mean by "merit," then a comparison to Article XI of our Confession of Faith reveals striking similarities. We are rewarded with the vision of God because of our fulfillment of God's commandments, even though this fulfillment itself is always an act of God's grace within which we can at most participate, and never generate from our own resources. Or as Article X in the Confession puts it, these good works that are the "necessary" fruit of justification are "pleasing to God," but they are not the basis for the right relationship we enjoy with God. Jesus' obedience alone is the source of that right relationship. For this reason we confess, "The offering Christ freely made on the cross is the perfect and sufficient sacrifice for the sins of the whole world, redeeming man from all sin, so that no other satisfaction is required."

Free Us for Joyful Obedience

The United Methodist basic worship service includes a prayer of confession. This is the prayer that allows us to move from our baptism to the Lord's Supper or the Eucharist. We should never go to the table without first confessing our sins and being forgiven, for as our article on sanctification states, without holiness we cannot properly see God. Sanctification "is the work of God's grace through the Word and the Spirit, by which those who have been born again are cleansed from sin in their thoughts, words and acts, and are enabled to live in accordance with God's will, and to strive for holiness without which no one will see the Lord." The prayer of confession effects such a cleansing. This is why we begin by confessing our sins, and then conclude by praying, "Forgive us, we pray. Free us for joyful obedience through Jesus Christ our Lord." The phrase "joyful obedience" states well the doctrine of sanctification. Sanctification is not some onerous observance of God's Law. If we find God's Law repressive and live by it only out of a sense of duty, then we are far from perfection. Joyful obedience names the perfection we seek. It is an ecstatic state of blessedness where our life becomes so taken up into God's life that following Christ brings joy and contentment. By being caught up in participation in God's life, we "are enabled, through grace, to love God with all our hearts and to walk in his holy commandments blameless." This is the heart of the Wesleyan tradition—"obedient love."

Perfection is to love as God loves. So how does God love? We find an answer in the article on sanctification, which shows God's love to be a work of both the Word and the Spirit. God's love is Trinitarian, and our participation in this love is a participation in Word and Spirit. God loves God's self such that God "gives" his own being away only to receive it again, which means God is one in three and three in one. We witnessed this amazing act of love and generosity in the doctrine of the Trinity and in the relationship between God and creation. That God is three Persons in One signifies that God is not an isolated, unitary being removed from relationship. God is in God's own self—relationality. The Son receives all the fullness of the divinity that the Father is and returns it to the Father. What makes the Father the Father is only that he is the Father of the Son. In other words, the Son's sonship makes the Father the Father. Likewise both the Father and the Son "process" the Holy Spirit. The fullness of the Father and the Son's divinity is given to the Holy Spirit, who likewise returns it to them as the Gift of Love that is the Spirit. This Gift gives us life, redeems us in the Son, and sustains us in the Christian life. The Spirit gives us life through the act of creation and new birth.

Creation is not necessary for God. God does not need it for God's own sake. There is no "being" outside of God upon which God works, trying to force it into God's own image. God does not need creation—and yet creation exists. How do we account for this? Creation is pure gift; it comes from nothing. This gift also underlies our redemption in Christ. The Spirit makes his mission possible; it comes upon him in baptism. But the Son also pours out the Spirit upon the Church to continue his work of reconciliation. The Spirit's presence in the Church sustains us in the Christian life; it makes possible obedient love, which is the basis for the Christian life.

Questions for Consideration:

1. What is unique about the Wesleyan understanding of justification and sanctification?

2. What is justification by faith? What is the difference between "imputed" and "imparted" righteousness?

3. How is justification a reckoning?

4. What is sanctification?

5. What does it mean to say that we are not only accounted righteous but we are made righteous?

6. What is the relationship and/or distinction between "imputed" righteousness and "inherent" righteousness?

7. What is regeneration?

8. What is the Wesleyan doctrine of perfection?

9. What are the dangers of misunderstanding the doctrine of perfection?

10. How are we to rightfully understand the doctrines of sanctification and perfection?

11. What are the consequences of understanding justification and sanctification for the wider church?

12. How do you describe joyful obedience?

13. How is "obedient love" the heart of the Wesleyan tradition?

nine

The Christian Life

Articles of Religion: Article VI: **Of the Old Testament**

The Old Testament is not contrary to the New; for both in the Old and New Testament everlasting life is offered to mankind by Christ, who is the only Mediator between God and man, being both God and Man. Wherefore they are not to be heard who feign that the old fathers did look only for transitory promises. Although the law given from God by Moses as touching ceremonies and rites doth not bind Christians, nor ought the civil precepts thereof of necessity be received in any commonwealth; yet notwithstanding, no Christian whatsoever is free from the obedience of the commandments which are called moral.

Articles of Religion: Article X: **Of Good Works**

Although good works, which are the fruits of faith, and follow after justification, cannot put away our sins, and endure the severity of God's judgment; yet are they pleasing and acceptable to God in Christ, and spring out of a true and lively faith, insomuch that by them a lively faith may be as evidently known as a tree is discerned by its fruit.

Articles of Religion: Article XI: **Of Works of Supererogation**

Voluntary works—besides, over and above God's commandments—which they call works of supererogation, cannot be taught without arrogancy and impiety. For by them men do declare that they do not only render unto God as much as they are bound to do, but that they do more for his sake than of bounden duty is re-

84

quired; whereas Christ saith plainly: When you have done all that is commanded you, say, We are unprofitable servants.

Articles of Religion: Article XII: **Of Sin after Justification**

Not every sin willingly committed after justification is the sin against the Holy Ghost, and unpardonable. Wherefore, the grant of repentance is not to be denied to such as fall into sin after justification. After we have received the Holy Ghost, we may depart from grace given, and fall into sin, and, by the grace of God, rise again and amend our lives. And therefore they are to be condemned who say they can no more sin as long as they live here; or deny the place of forgiveness to such as truly repent.

Articles of Religion: Article XXIII: **Of the Rulers of the United States of America**

The President, the Congress, the general assemblies, the governors, and the councils of state, as the delegates of the people, are the rulers of the United States of America, according to the division of power made to them by the Constitution of the United States and by the constitutions of their respective states. And the said states are a sovereign and independent nation, and ought not to be subject to any foreign jurisdiction.

Articles of Religion: Article XXIV: **Of Christian Men's Goods**

The riches and goods of Christians are not common as touching the right, title, and possession of the same, as some do falsely boast. Notwithstanding, every man ought, of such things as he possesseth, liberally to give alms to the poor, according to his ability.

Confession of Faith: Article X: **Good Works**

We believe good works are the necessary fruits of faith and follow regeneration but they do not have the virtue to remove our sins or to avert divine judgment. We believe good works, pleasing and acceptable to God in Christ, spring from a true and living faith, for through and by them faith is made evident.

Confession of Faith: Article XVI: **Civil Government**

We believe civil government derives its just powers from the sovereign God. As Christians we recognize the government under whose protection we reside and believe such government should be based on, and be responsible for, the recognition of human rights under God. We believe war and bloodshed are contrary to the gospel and spirit of Christ. We believe it is the duty of Christian citizens to give moral strength and purpose to their respective governments through sober, righteous and godly living.

W hat is obedient love? To answer that question we must look to the Old Testament and the role of the Law. Article VI of the Articles of Religion indicates how the Law functions.

Ceremonial, Civil, and Moral Laws

Article VI begins by making a traditional threefold distinction in the Law: it is ceremonial, civil, or moral. There are those laws that touch on ceremonies, such as what you should eat and what you shouldn't, and whether or not males should be circumcised. These ceremonial laws are no longer in effect for Christians. Peter's vision in Acts 10 and Paul's mission to the Gentiles led to a rereading of these obligations. Christians are permitted to eat all things, and they need not be circumcised. In fact, baptism replaces circumcision as the "ceremonial" obligation imposed upon Christians, opening the covenant to both men and women in a new way.

There are also "civil precepts" that provide legal obligations for how God's people should love, such as Sabbath observance or the Jubilee Year in Leviticus 25. These civil precepts are not to be imposed upon any particular nation or state. We need not force the Ten Commandments upon the nation-state's judicial system. The Wesleyan tradition recognizes with Saint Augustine that there are two cities that coexist until Christ returns— the earthly city and the City of God. The obligation we owe to the earthly city is "to give moral strength and purpose . . . through sober, righteous and godly living." This is similar to a famous claim made by St. Augustine in his book *The City of God*, in which he wrote,

> The heavenly city, while it sojourns on earth . . . not scrupling about diversities in the manners, laws, and institutions whereby earthly peace is secured and maintained, but recognizing that, however various these are, they all tend to one and the same end of earthly peace . . . [is] so far from rescinding and abolishing these

diversities, that it even preserves and adopts them so long only as no hindrance to the worship of the one supreme and true God is thus introduced. Even the heavenly city, therefore, while in its state of pilgrimage, avails itself of the peace of earth, and . . . desires and maintains a common agreement among men regarding the acquisition of the necessities of life so far as it can without injuring faith and godliness.[1]

We live in the midst of two cities. We should not try to impose the obligations of the City of God on the earthly city; nor should the City of God accommodate the earthly city's "secular" ways. Instead, we recognize that the two cities can make alliances even while we acknowledge their diversity. However, any such alliance has two important qualifications. If they hinder the true worship of God or injure faith and godliness, then Christians can make no alliance. This is why right worship is such an important political act for the Christian life.

Obedient love does not require observing certain ceremonial laws. Nor does it require imposing the Old Testament's civil precepts upon the nation-state. But it does require that we keep inviolate the "moral precepts." This traditional threefold distinction between ceremonial, civil, and moral precepts is difficult to determine with any precision. What makes something moral rather than ceremonial or civil? Our church's recent debates and potential division over sexual practices shows how difficult this distinction is to determine. Is the traditional understanding of sexual activity as a lifelong, monogamous relationship between a man and a woman part of the moral precept that must continue to be honored? Or does it fall under those ceremonial or even civil precepts that are no longer binding? This debate, like all debates over ethical and political matters in the church, is finally a debate over the question of holiness.

Holiness

Obedient love is holiness, and Christians, like Jews, are summoned to respond to God's gracious initiative by sanctifying Gods' Name and thereby making God's creation holy. We sanctify God's creation by living obediently to the Law through the power of faith. We discussed the first table

---

1. Augustine, *City of God*, bk. 19, ch. 17.

of the Law in the first lesson. It directs us to the love of God and includes these commandments:

1. I am the Lord your God; you shall not have strange gods before me.

2. You shall not take the name of the Lord your God in vain.

3. Remember to keep holy the Lord's Day.

The second table of the Law directs us to the love of neighbor. It includes these commandments:

4. Honor your father and mother.

5. You shall not kill.

6. You shall not commit adultery.

7. You shall not steal.

8. You shall not bear false witness against your neighbor.

9. You shall not covet your neighbor's wife or husband.

10. You shall not covet your neighbor's goods.

The Wesleyan tradition recognizes the importance of these laws and seeks to establish them through faith. In fact, many of these commands are found in our General Rules. Faith establishes the Law and directs us to the love of neighbor.

Establishing the Law through Faith

Mr. Wesley wrote an important sermon titled "The Law Established through Faith." Following many other theologians who came before him, he did not set the law in opposition to grace and faith. True faith lives the law and in so doing "sanctifies" God's Name on earth. This is our most basic prayer, "Our Father, who art in heaven, hallowed be your Name." To hallow God's Name is to sanctify it. It is to pray, "May your Name be made holy." This is done by living in accordance with God's wisdom and will. It is obedient love, which is "to love God with all our hearts and to walk in his holy commandments blameless," as our article on sanctification states. Prior to Mr. Wesley's sermon on "The Law Established through Faith," he wrote thirteen discourses on the Sermon on the Mount. These discourses are important for any Wesleyan understanding of the Christian life, for they set forth what he meant by "the religion of the heart." In fact, he explains why he wrote and published his sermons, which are also part of our established standards of doctrine. In the 1746 preface to his *Sermons*, he stated:

> And herein it is more especially my desire, first, to guard those who are just setting their faces toward heaven (and who, having little acquaintance with the things of God, are the more liable to be turned out of the way) from formality, from mere outside religion, which has almost driven heart-religion out of the world; and secondly, to warn those who know the religion of the heart, the faith which worketh by love, lest at any time they make void the law through faith, and so fall back into the snare of the devil.[2]

Wesley's sermons have a twofold concern. First he guards against a "formality" in the Christian life. This would be pure ceremony where we think that the mere outward observance of the sacraments, an external affirmation of the orthodox creeds, and a willingness not to violate the law are sufficient. We could do all these things and, as Luther taught, still not fulfill the law "spiritually." This is insufficient. But nor is it sufficient to think that once we have the religion of the heart, we can do without these external formalities, without proper sacramental worship, orthodox creeds, or the law. Thus Wesley has a second concern that those who claim to know the religion of the heart do not "make void the law through faith, and so fall back into the snare of the devil."

On the one hand, we should not make the law, ritual, and doctrine ends in themselves. Then we have mere formality. On the other hand, we should not think that once we have the religion of the heart we no longer need law, ritual, or doctrine. Let me explain this with an example. Imagine I have a difficult neighbor and I wake up every day debating whether or not I should kill my neighbor. I do a cost-benefit analysis, weighing the benefits I would receive from the costs. If I kill my neighbor, he will no longer be able to annoy me. But there will be costs. I might be sent to jail, which would end my career as a professional religious person. So after weighing the costs against the benefits, I decide not to kill my neighbor. Then the question arises, have I kept the Law? Have I kept the sixth com-

2. Wesley, *Works*, 1:106.

mandment—"Thou shalt not kill"? The answer is yes and no. Yes, I kept the law in a purely formal manner. I did not do the thing I wanted to do. I did not kill my neighbor. If someone decided to keep the law only in this purely formal manner and chose not to kill me, I would nonetheless be grateful. Such merely external observances are better than the alternative. Yet I have not truly kept the Law. I have not observed what matters most. I am summoned by God's Law to love my neighbor. If I am truly free for joyful obedience, it would not even occur to me to do a cost-benefit analysis to determine whether or not I should kill my neighbor. If I have the "religion of the heart," and then claim that I can go about breaking the law because it no longer has a hold on my life, then I have "made void the law through faith."

The above example from the Law could be replaced with doctrine and the sacraments and the point would be similar. If I claim to have the religion of the heart, and therefore no longer hold to right doctrine or think I no longer need the sacraments and proper Christian worship, then I make void the Law through faith. But if I cling to right doctrine and proper Christian worship as a mere formality, believing that it alone is what truly matters, then I possess only an empty formality and not the religion of the heart.

The Religion of the Heart

What is this religion of the heart? It is good works. Good works are the fruit of faith. As Article X of our Articles of Religion states, good works are "pleasing and acceptable to God in Christ, and spring out of a true and lively faith, insomuch that by them a lively faith may be as evidently known as a tree is discerned by its fruit." This fruit is the "beatitude" or "happiness" that Jesus pronounces as the true end of the Law in his Sermon on the Mount.

In the Sermon on the Mount, Jesus is presented to us in a manner very similar to Moses. As Moses was on the mount receiving the Law, so Jesus is on the mount giving the purpose of the Law. For Christians, these are not two distinct events that can be divided from each other. The Law given to Moses is God's mediation of God's wisdom and will to creation. For this reason, Christians will always see in it the life of Jesus. Article VI clearly states this: "The Old Testament is not contrary to the New; for both in the Old and New Testament everlasting life is offered to mankind by Christ, who is the only Mediator between God and man, being both God and Man." Because of this single Mediator, Wesley referred to Jesus as the Torah of God. Christians must read the Old Testament christologically; we find Jesus in it. This is why, following Wesley, I have capitalized "Law."

Before he begins to explain the importance of the religion of the heart as disclosed in the Sermon on the Mount, Wesley states the importance of recognizing who it is that is speaking: "Let us observe who it is that is here speaking that we may 'take heed how we hear' . . . It speaks the Creator of all—a God, a God appears! Yea, [the One Who Is], the being of all beings, Jehovah, the self-existent, the supreme, the God who is over all, blessed for ever."[3] Jesus speaks and gives us the purpose of the Law. It is found in "beatitude" or happiness. In the Sermon on the Mount, Jesus pronounces certain ways of life blessed. These are the eight beatitudes. Throughout the Christian tradition, these beatitudes were correlated with the gifts of the Holy Spirit to give us a sense of what the Christian life should look like.

The beatitudes are: poverty of spirit, meekness, mourning, righteousness, mercifulness, purity of heart, peaceableness, and persecution for righteousness' sake. The gifts are fear, pity, knowledge, fortitude, counsel, understanding, and wisdom. Many great theologians of the church, such as St. Augustine and St. Thomas Aquinas, correlated the first seven beatitudes with the first seven gifts. Mr. Wesley did something quite similar. This helps us understand why these good works are the "fruit" of the Holy Spirit. They are not first and foremost our own works; we cannot produce them by ourselves. They are the "fruit" of our reconciliation with God and our neighbor, a reconciliation that the Holy Spirit effects in our lives. This helps us understand two important teachings in our established doctrines. First, we are not to trust in our own good works and think they can redeem us. This is why our Confession, Article X, states, "We believe good works are the necessary fruits of faith and follow regeneration but they do not have the virtue to remove our sins or to avert divine judgment." Second, once we understand that good works are the "fruit" of faith, we acknowledge that we cannot be redeemed without them. For this reason, Article X states: "Although good works, which are the fruits of

3. Wesley, *Works*, 1:474.

faith, and follow after justification, cannot put away our sins, and endure the severity of God's judgment; yet are they pleasing and acceptable to God in Christ, and spring out of a true and lively faith, insomuch that by them a lively faith may be as evidently known as a tree is discerned by its fruit." Good works do not redeem us, but they are "pleasing" and "acceptable" to God. In fact, as Matthew 25 teaches, they will be the basis for judgment in the Last Day.

In the Sermon on the Mount, Jesus shows us the goal of the Christian life. This is the form of life he will bless on the Last Day. Our response to this life of beatitude or blessedness should at least include three elements. First, we should recognize that only One Person ever lived this blessed way of life by his own agency. Jesus is the only one who embodied the fullness of righteousness found in the beatitudes. As often happens in a world in rebellion against God and God's goodness, such a perfect performance ended in his persecution even unto death. Those who fully embody the first seven beatitudes will often receive the "gift" of the eighth. The church is built on the blood of the martyrs. Second, we must seek to embody his righteousness in our own life. This is what it means to confess that "the Lord is our righteousness." It means more than a purely external imputation of righteousness; it also entails an inherent sanctifying righteousness. Third, we should honor those who embody these ways of life and hold them up as examples to be emulated, recognizing that such a righteousness must be socially enacted. It is not only for individuals.

Just as the doctrines of our church are the communal norms for how we should think and teach, so the beatitudes and gifts are the communal norms for how we should live. Whenever and wherever we find the fruits of peaceableness, righteousness, mercy, and so on, we should recognize a proper performance of the grace of the Holy Spirit. We should not be surprised, then, or dismiss it as the politicization of our doctrinal standards, when we discover that our standards speak about matters such as how Methodists should think about war and economics. For instance, Article XVI states that we believe war and bloodshed are contrary to the gospel and spirit of Jesus. This is not a private judgment; it is a public confession that reminds us that the religion of the heart requires a political embodiment in how we think about matters like participation in war, economics, family life, and the government. We cannot assess how we should live in these important social institutions without keeping our vision on the way of life Christ announces as blessed. This vision must be the focus of the Christian life and the source of our evangelistic witness to the world.

When the Methodist movement began, its adherents covenanted to live their lives by three "General Rules": Do no harm, do good, and attend upon the ordinances of God. Under each of these rules are a number of specific rules, some negative (refusing to own slaves, to take a brother or sister to court, or to use costly apparel) and others positive (celebrating the Lord's Supper frequently and giving of our money to the poor). The General Rules are to guide us toward the blessed life. They remain in our Discipline today and, in theory, are binding on everyone who joins the United Methodist Church. But much like the neglect of the teaching found in our Confession and Articles of Religion, so many Methodists do not know we are bound together in a covenant of General Rules. They should be studied and translated into a present-day idiom by all Wesleyan Christians.[4] However, these rules are not ends in themselves; they are means that should be used to cultivate the religion of the heart. We must avoid both mere formality—keeping the rules for their own sake—and making void the law through faith—rejecting the rules as irrelevant for present-day Christian life.

Lest we think that the Wesleyan doctrines of justification, sanctification, and perfection lead to a state where Christians can be complacent and think they have "arrived" in their Christian life, we must always remember the importance of our Article XII, "Of Sin after Justification":

> Not every sin willingly committed after justification is the sin against the Holy Ghost, and unpardonable. Wherefore, the grant of repentance is not to be denied to such as fall into sin after justification. After we have received the Holy Ghost, we may depart from grace given, and fall into sin, and, by the grace of God, rise again and amend our lives. And therefore they are to be condemned who say they can no more sin as long as they live here; or deny the place of forgiveness to such as truly repent.

The Christian life is a life of ongoing repentance. No one can proceed in it without continuing to repent and turn to Christ each day of her or his

---

4. For an excellent example and use of this, see Michael Cartwright and Andrew Kinsey's *Watching Over One Another in Love: Reclaiming the Wesleyan Rule of Life for the Church's Mission.*

life. The theologian Hans Urs von Balthasar reminded us that the teaching of Jesus requires both a rigorousness and a leniency at the same time. Each new day brings the promise of fresh forgiveness for making the law void, as well as the hope of living into the Triune life through Christ.

Questions for Consideration:

1. What is the threefold distinction of the law?

2. What is the relationship between the city of God and the earthly city?

3. What was John Wesley's twofold concern about the Christian life?

4. What is the way we make the law void?

5. What is the connection between God the lawgiver and the life of blessedness?

6. What is the Wesleyan understanding of the relationship between faith and works?

7. What are the three elements of blessedness?

8. What is the relationship between the life of blessedness and the General Rules?

9. What are the General Rules?

10. How do you—your church—keep the General Rules?

ten

Judgment

Confession of Faith: Article XII: **The Judgment and the Future State**

We believe all men stand under the righteous judgment of Jesus Christ, both now and in the last day. We believe in the resurrection of the dead; the righteous to life eternal and the wicked to endless condemnation.

M r. Wesley began the Methodist movement in order to help people "flee from the wrath to come." This was the reason he gave for forming the people called Methodist. Wesleyans originated from a palpable sense of Christ's final judgment. But this initial reason for Methodism's existence is as far from contemporary Methodism as riding horses is from flying airplanes. We no longer exist to help people flee from the wrath to come; on the whole, we do not anticipate Christ's final judgment. There are good reasons for this. Many Christians grew tired of sermons that focused only on hell and damnation, the whole emphasis of which was avoiding this fate. Such preaching lost the positive focus of directing our lives toward beatitude and became content with the negative focus of avoiding evil. It forgot that to stand under Christ's judgment is to stand beneath him on the Mount and to hear the forms of life he pronounces as blessed. This is a judgment that gives life rather than takes it away.

But there are also less than good reasons for why Methodists lost a public presentation on the doctrine of judgment. It makes us uncomfortable to raise questions of how we and others do and should live. In a culture filled with sentimental self-acceptance, we seek a "god" who never raises such questions but always affirms us in what we do. In 1937, H. Richard Niebuhr penned his memorable indictment of Christianity in the United States, where "a God without wrath brought men without sin into a kingdom without judgment through the ministrations of a Christ without a cross."[1] Fifty years later, Martin Marty wrote an essay for the Harvard Theological Review, the title of which said it all: "Hell Disappeared. No One Noticed . . ." (1985). Mainline Protestant churches lost any sense of judgment. We are uncomfortable discussing it.

Christ: The Righteous Judge

The first thing to remember about our teaching on the judgment is whose judgment it is. Our Confession is quite explicit on this question: "We believe all men stand under the righteous judgment of Jesus Christ, both now and in the last day." The One who judges is Jesus, and he will judge with a "righteous judgment," not the dishonest or hypocritical judgment we would rightly fear. It is not a judgment that should catch us by surprise, for we already witnessed it in the Sermon on the Mount. The second thing to remember is that judgment is for the purpose of resurrection. Christians believe in the resurrection of the body. We do not believe in the flight of the soul from the body. In fact, the true Christian vision of the end of time is that of a new heaven and a new earth. Because God's creation is good, God intends to restore it and make a place for it within God's own life. This will be an act of God's creative power where God brings new life out of that which has turned to dust—including our dead bodies. The vision is that of John:

> Then I saw a new heaven and a new earth; for the first heaven and the first earth had passed away, and the sea was no more. And I saw the holy city, the new Jerusalem, coming down out of heaven from God, prepared as a bride adorned for her husband. (Rev 21:1–2)

---

1. Niebuhr, *The Kingdom of God in America*, 193.

The Holy City

Christ's judgment is for the sake of the city of God. It is a city where peace, justice, and harmony will reign. For this reason, the vision includes a judgment against those who cannot live by the blessed way of life to which Christ points.

> But as for the cowardly, the faithless, the polluted, the murderers, the fornicators, the sorcerers, the idolaters, and all liars, their place will be in the lake that burns with fire and sulfur, which is the second death. (Rev 21:8)

This is poetic imagery that reveals to us the reason for our redemption. Through his ascension, Christ alone is given authority to judge. We do not have the power to send anyone to hell. Christ's judgment will not be arbitrary, but based upon what is necessary for us to live in his "city" as he intends. This is a city whose bonds are founded upon what is noble, true, good, and charitable rather than upon mere power and will. And this is the sole reason for the judgment. It makes possible a city founded solely upon holiness, upon God's glory, something which is not easy for fallen creatures to accept and is the reason Christ makes himself the sacrifice that establishes this city.

St. Thomas Aquinas, following St. Augustine, makes this explicit in his doctrine of hell and damnation. He writes, "sin renders a person worthy to be altogether cut off from the fellowship of God's city, and this is the effect of every sin committed against charity, which is the bond uniting this same city together."[2] This is a reference to the expulsion from the garden. Because hatred and arbitrariness cannot be the true basis for social life, hell is a possibility. It is expulsion from God's holy city. Hell is the judgment against our unwillingness to forge substantive bonds of our life together through charity. Because our evil actions have social consequences that outlast us and our intentions, a final judgment is necessary to restore the bonds of charity that alone make creation possible and alone can be eternal. In his discussion of the "final judgment," Aquinas says that we must have a final judgment—and not just a judgment at our deaths—

---

2. Aquinas, *Summa Theologica*, Q. 99, art. 1, 203.

because our sin, like our faithfulness, bears social consequences that must be redeemed if we are to live in God's city.[3]

The Judgment

In his sermon "The Great Assize," Mr. Wesley takes as his text Romans 14:10: "We shall all stand before the judgment seat of Christ." Because he is "of God," Jesus receives the authority to judge. Since all of Wesley's theology is based on our return into the Image of God, this is not simply a pious throwaway line. As the only true Image of the Father, Jesus is the one who both reveals all that the Father is and makes possible our return to him. He is the full and definitive manifestation of God such that no other is needed. As the Second Person of the Trinity, the Son is not simply some act of will that God chooses, which could be other. He is the very Truth and Wisdom of God who discloses God's Perfections. God's "freedom" is not to choose whether or not to be Triune; God is Triune. This is God's omnipotence. It is also God's truth and goodness. Thus it must manifest itself, not out of a capricious act of will, but because of the Truth itself. It cannot be other. This requires judgment. As Wesley says,

> . . . it is apparently and absolutely necessary, for the full display of the glory of God, for the clear and perfect manifestation of his wisdom, justice, power and mercy toward the heirs of salvation, that all circumstances of their life should be placed in open view, together with all their tempers, and all the desires, thoughts and intents of their hearts. Otherwise how would it appear out of what a depth of sin and misery the grace of God had delivered them? And, indeed, if the whole lives of all the children of men were not manifestly discovered, the whole amazing contexture of divine providence could not be manifested . . . And then only when God hath brought to light all the hidden things of darkness, whosoever were the actors therein, will it be seen that wise and good were all his ways; that he "saw through the thick cloud" and governed all things by the wise "counsel of his own will"; that nothing was left to chance or the caprice of men, but God disposed all "strongly and sweetly," and wrought all into one connected chain of justice, mercy and truth.[4]

3. Aquinas, *Summa Theologica* III. 59 art. 5.
4. Wesley, *Works*, 1:364–65.

Note several important claims Wesley makes here. First, judgment is a manifestation of God's glory. It is not an incentive for us to be moral. Instead, it brings to light what God has already done, who God always is. Second, by bringing to light our wickedness, God does not damn us but shows forth his own wisdom. We discover that even though it seemed that life was simply capricious, in fact God knit the world together through justice, mercy, and truth and not arbitrary will. What is the result of the judgment? Wesley tells us that it is "the discovery of the divine perfections." This returns us to our very first lesson. In the judgment we learn God's Name and, in so doing, God's Name is sanctified. Our sins are the lack of what God possesses in full. This is grace, for our perfection does not depend on us securing our own perfection by our own resources, but on our participating in God's perfections. This is why the righteous "rejoice" in the revelation of God's perfections. Wesley writes, "And in the discovery of the divine perfections the righteous will rejoice with joy unspeakable; far from feeling any painful sorrow or shame for any of those past transgressions which were long since blotted out as a cloud washed away by the blood of the Lamb."[5]

In the light of God's glory, that perfect splendor of luminosity that blinds from its brilliance, human creation cannot but be judged and therefore purified and sanctified. This must occur because we cannot see God unless we are made like God—perfect. Note how Wesley assumes that human sin is subordinate to God's perfections: "only when God hath brought to light all the hidden things of darkness, whosoever were the actors therein, will it be seen that wise and good were all his ways." God's perfections are the true ground of our being. They lack nothing, and thus God needs nothing from us. Sin, then, is a mere lack that poses no threat to God and is not necessary for human existence. It must and can be judged precisely because God's perfections are the true norm. In that sense, hell would not be outside of God, for as we already mentioned, there can be no "outside" of God. Hell is that place God makes for those who refuse to live as faithful citizens of God's Holy City, those who never admit that human community can be forged by the bonds of charity and not simply through arbitrary will.

5. Ibid., 365.

Who will be included and who excluded in this city? We do not know. This means that we cannot determine who is in and who is out. In fact, as the theologian Hans Urs von Balthasar reminded us, Holy Scripture sets forth two series of statements that could potentially be read as contradictory.[6] One series speaks of the threat of judgment and the possibility of a loss for all eternity: Matt 5:22, 29ff.; 8:12; 10:28; 22:11ff; 23:33; 25:30; Mark 9:43; 19:20; 20:10; 21:18. The other series speaks of God's will and ability to save all: 1 Tim 2:1–6; John 12:32; 17:2; Rom 5:12–21; 11:32; and especially 1 Tim 2:4. Our mission is not to speculate on who is in and who is out, but to prepare ourselves by learning to live in anticipation of that Holy City which God prepares for us in Christ. When we get preoccupied with "universalism" or "eternal damnation," we miss what matters most and assume God's seat of judgment for ourselves. What matters most? That through Christ's active and righteous obedience we live into the Triune life and, having been justified, also take on that righteousness that is Christ's own and make it ours in order to make God's Name holy and give God the glory. What other reason could God possibly have for raising up Wesleyan Christianity?

Questions for Consideration:

1. Who is the Judge?

2. What explains the discomfort with the topic of judgment?

3. What are important points to keep in mind with judgment?

4. What problems traditionally surface when discussing judgment and the future?

5. What does it mean to confess that we believe in "righteous judgment"?

6. How do we understand the wrath to come? Is this spoken of in your church?

7. How do we understand the Holy City?

8. What are the important claims John Wesley makes concerning God's judgment?

---

6. Von Balthasar, *Dare We Hope that All Men Be Saved?*, 21.

9. How do you understand heaven and hell? What is heaven? What is hell?

10. How do we understand the future state? What is it?

11. What other questions remain for you as you complete this study/commentary? What next steps may you need to take?

Bibliography

Augustine. *City of God*. Translated by Marcus Dodds. Grand Rapids: Eerdmans, 1979.

Balthasar, Hans Urs Von. *Dare We Hope that All Men Be Saved?* San Francisco: Ignatius, 1988.

Basil, Saint, Bishop of Caesarea. *On the Holy Spirit*. Translated by David Anderson. Crestwood, NY: St. Vladimir's Seminary Press, 1980.

"By Water and the Holy Spirit: A United Methodist Understanding of Baptism." Online: http://archives.umc.org/interior_print.asp?ptid=4&mid=992.

Cartwright, Michael, and Andrew Kinsey. *Watching Over One Another in Love: Reclaiming the Wesleyan Rule of Life for the Church's Mission*. Eugene, OR: Wipf & Stock Publishers, 2011.

Congar, Yves. *I Believe in the Holy Spirit*. Vol. 2, *"He Is Lord and Giver of Life."* Translated by David Smith. New York: Seabury, 1983.

Luther, Martin. *Martin Luther: Selections from His Writings*. Edited by John Dillenberger. Garden City, NY: Doubleday, 1961.

Niebuhr, H. Richard. *The Kingdom of God in America*. Middletown, CT: Wesleyan Universtity Press, 1988.

"This Holy Mystery: A United Methodist Understanding of Holy Communion." Online: http://www.kintera.org/atf/cf/%7B3482e846-598f-460a-b9a7-386734470eda%7D/THM-BYGC.PDF.

The United Methodist Hymnal: Book of United Methodist Worship. Nashville: United Methodist Publishing House, 1989.

Wainwright, Geoffrey. *Doxology: The Praise of God in Worship, Doctrine, and Life: A Systematic Theology*. New York: Oxford University Press, 1980.

———. "The Holy Spirit." In *The Cambridge Companion to Christian Doctrine*, edited by Colin Gunton, 273–96. Cambridge: Cambridge University Press, 1997.

Wesley, John. *The Works of John Wesley*. Bicentennial ed. Edited by Albert C. Outler. Nashville: Abingdon, 1984–.

Wright, N. T. *The Last Word: Scripture and the Authority of God—Getting beyond the Bible Wars*. New York: HarperCollins, 2005.